son___

SPRING/SUMMER 2023

CW01371099

IDENTITY

Issue VII brought to you by Sonder Magazine
Co-editors: Sinéad Creedon and Orla Murphy
Cover artwork: © Martins Deep
Printing services: Sooner Than Later,
24 Kill Avenue, Dun Laoghaire, Co Dublin

ISBN: 978 1 39994 612 4

Sonder Magazine is proud to be
funded by Arts Council Ireland

Website: sonderlit.com
Facebook: @sonderlit
Twitter: @MagazineSonder
Instagram: @sonder_lit

sonder

The realisation that each passerby
has a life as complex as your own.

EDITOR'S NOTE

Welcome back to the seventh issue of *Sonder Magazine*. We are thrilled to bring you yet another issue packed to the brim with completely original and exciting works.

You might have noticed, but this issue has undergone a teeny tiny rebrand. We decided we wanted to focus exclusively on previously undiscovered writers, offering a platform for them to jump from, and spotlighting them as well as we possibly can. You'll find that each writer in this issue is emerging, apart from our featured writer, who we are super excited to have on board: Sue Rainsford.

Issue VII opens with a brand new piece by the highly acclaimed author of *Follow Me to Ground* and *Redder Days*, and we even got the chance to sit down with Sue and get some tips and tricks for aspiring writers. Hopefully you or the writer in your life will find some solace and inspiration in her words. This is a feature we hope to bring forward into the future, and it wouldn't have been possible without the generous support of Arts Council Ireland.

That's right – you read that right! This is our first year receiving funding, which means that we are finally able to pay writers fairly and transparently. Up until this issue, every penny we made went towards paying our contributors, which meant we could never guarantee a deserved sum. I would like to take this moment to say that the only reason *Sonder* still exists today is because of you, the reader, and you, the writer, for continuing to pick up a copy, submit to our issues, engage with us online, and show face at our events. Really, the reason we do it is for you. From the bottom of our hearts, thank you for sticking with us.

The theme of this issue is Identity – something that everyone, no matter what corner of the world you're in or how you align yourself, can relate to. We hope we can, through the power of the written word, connect us all together.

XO
S&O

CONTENTS

1	**BODY OF INK** By Sue Rainsford	25	**WAR MAKER** By E J DELANEY
5	**AN HOURGLASS AND HER STRIPES** By Kirsten Mosher	32	**DARK HOURS** By Ian Ledward
7	**THE SHUDDERING CREAK OF TIME** By Patrick Kruth	39	**SCABBED KNUCKLES** By Chris Kuriata
12	**THE INDICTMENT OF ROBERT FROST** By Kayla King	42	**DAMSELFLY** By Epiphany Ferrell
19	**A CLOVEN HOOF** By Sam Martone	43	**WINDMILL** By Justin Clement
23	**CARTOGRAPHY** By Aisling Cahill	50	**CHESTER BEATTY'S LONELY HEARTS CLUB BAND** By Sahar Ahmed

54	**THE SILENT WOMAN** By Olivia Payne	86	**WAYWARD SUN** By Isa Robertson
60	**WINDOW** By Justin Rigamonti	89	**FAR SIDE OF THE MOON** By Colm Brennan
61	**AND ALSO WITH YOU** By Lea Mc Carthy	92	**BENVOLIO'S SECRET** By Valerie Hunter
65	**EXTRAORDINARY** By Don Noel	94	**THE HUNGRY BOG** By Robert Coakley
71	**TIDES** By Claire O'Brien	103	**IN CONVERSATION WITH SUE RAINSFORD**
78	**THE CROWD** By Robert Coakley	114	**ABOUT THE CONTRIBUTORS**
84	**ANTS FROM UP HERE** By Cian Dunne		

FEATURED WRITER

BODY OF INK

By Sue Rainsford

(I)

In the dense brush, a pale creature squats low and bites into the meat of her forearm. All around her, tall trees drop their heavy fruit.

She knows that it is dusk and that the coming night will be a cool one. Knows, too, that the clouds are teeming with rain that will fall and scent the ready earth.

What she doesn't know: when the rain is done the freshly turned soil will keep soft a long time. Soft enough, that in the middle of the night when it comes time to lie on her side she'll imprint the giving loam with her haunch, hip and rib.

Something else she doesn't know: the svelte curve she'll leave behind in the rain-rich ground will be the root of a word and that word is 'woman'.

This word she plants in the dirt: it means any two-legged mammal that knows the taste of her own sweet flesh—who eats of her own arm though the ground is rolling with fruit and the fruit is furred and edible.

When she wakes in the early morning, she wades into a body of water and its surface quickens while she gulps and bathes. If she had the time and the means to read them, she'd know what the ripples say. Would know, too, that they gather into the same question each and every day.

Who are you?

A breeze comes through—the ferric tang is a sign she should start running and so she does. She runs fast enough that the world begins to blur.

She doesn't know that with every loping mile she further infuses the word she left seeded behind her; after a thousand steps, it means any strong-limbed animal that moves with a mind to sink her teeth into the horizon. Any sleek-pelted mammal that looks at that hazy, distant line and sees the soft neck of the world and knows she must spend her days chasing it down with her strong jaw gripped closed.

She can feel it already, where earth kisses sky: she can feel it across the back of her tongue where it'll settle like a belt of flesh.

Any moment, now, she'll taste it; she need only take another step.

One more.

And another, and another—

(II)

A woman is writing in a room where morning sun shores up the walls. Behind her, a window looks onto a street and the street's noises bleed into the marks she makes on the page. The marks are made of ink and each one is a gift and a loss, both: something is returned to her at the exact moment something else is stripped away and she can't help but rock to and fro in her seat, a little, with the shifting weight of this unseen scale.

What this woman knows: where other women have a flexing thumb, she has a tough and grisled piece of meat and it will ache at the end of the day.

What she doesn't know: this aching sweep of muscle is the root of a word and that word is 'writer'. A word that means any woman who picks up a pen in order to carve and scratch and cut, who judges her day's work by how scattered the floor is with flayed wood and shards of stone.

Of the thousand marks she's made today, most won't survive the page—tomorrow she'll cross some out, put others aside to slowly fade.

Now, she stands up—hours of sitting have marked her ribcage with a swathe of red, wettish lace that shrinks and flexes before settling into the same seven words as every other day.

Are you who you want to be?

Who she is: a woman drunk on blue-black ink.

All day, she sips and sips while the sun does laps of the horizon and roves her back with its constant, clement heat.

(III)

In the curtained dark of an upstairs room a writer lies on her side. Outside, the sun is slow to rise and the moon lingers in partial outline. Inside, the air is thick with milk because milk has been spilled across its every threshold; on warmer days it settles as a curdled streak like a line of salt intended to keep cruel spirits at bay.

Her time in this room has taught her she has to lie very still so as not to set her body leaking, but she lets slip warm liquids all the same.

Now, a white droplet trails her side and—from the midst of the wakeful dreams that can only take hold in the dim morning—she believes she's been pierced by an arrow; she is a maimed soldier in an ancient war or a certain devout saint. In the weak dawn, the droplet moves towards a small face that has been sleeping in the nested sheets beside her.

More than the hot-tipped arrow, more than the moat of gold encircling the bed or the perching dragon cub who tucks its wings and gulps to stifle a ball of flame, she cannot believe this face is not a dream. This face that, in order to look at her, tilts its penny-sized chin and sets rolling a current that shakes the bed, that crackles the leaves and puckers the place where sky meets earth with a deep and sudden crease.

If there is a skybound god, this inclined chin has knocked him to his knees while the droplet slips further, falls—hits the sheets.

What the writer doesn't know: the pale trace yet to dry on the soft meat of her hip is the root of a word and that word is 'mother'.

This word—one of so many stains whorling the sheets—means any writer who comes to know the weight of her sore torso afloat milk-rushed linen. It means a writer with a palm cupped to her breast which is whitely weeping while she squints at the lines she tells herself are appearing beside her in the bed; who convinces herself she can see a looping, sodden script.

Who are you turning into?

Outside, the moon relents. The sun makes her golden claim on the sky.

Inside, to and fro, small blue eyes are sliding: they are their own cool planets and between them the cosmos sits suspended in a taut, glittering line.

(IV)

The sky is grey and pleated and a mother is walking a stretch of coast. Every step she took in walking here reminded her that where other women have a womb she has a pouch of silk and its seams are torn. They'd torn further by the time she'd arrived at this place where seaweed straggles rock; her pelvis is humming with blood ready to rush her legs and line her soles.

But—she knows it's a rare mother whose red prints haven't marked her path to spitting surf, who hasn't stood facing salted water and left behind a fragrant spoor. A rarer mother, still, who hasn't seen shapes etched on the high rocks, shapes by turn hidden and revealed by the rinsing foam and are in fact three, four words. Words written in chalk—no, they're made of ancient shards of bone: the splintered remnants of amoeba that gathered just so, waiting for a mother to come and stand here. A mother mad with thirst for words reading one, then another, struggling to make them out in full.

Who—become—

In the dense brush to her left, something jolts: something loping and assured. She can only guess at its shape because in moving it begins to blur, but she knows that the coarse growth closing over its quick haunch is the root of a word and that the word is 'creature'.

Knows, too, that this word will bud flowers and grow thorns. That it will soon mean any woman who lives with her nose in the trail of what it is her heart desires.

She'd like to take a thousand steps in the wake of this supple body but—too quickly—she's winded. Feels an old wound made freshly tender in her side. Instead, she calls out while there's a chance she might still be heard, asks to be told things that may or may not be lies.

I'll be waiting for you where dirt rubs against skyline.

You'll grow to fit the weight of a pen in your hand and the miracle of your unlikely child.

Yours is a body of ink, and it won't run dry.

(V)

One more step, and then another.

Some fast, some slow.

But every one is forward, forward.

On and on, toward the pressed lips of cloud and loam.

Across the back of her tongue, something settling.

A warm bead of milk; dispersed.

A cool shard of ink-stained stone.

AN HOURGLASS AND HER STRIPES

By Kirsten Mosher

An Hourglass
    He asks for an hour.

Her Stripes
    She is shaped like an hourglass. He paints stripes. He says he likes her androgynous look. He asks her to model for him. An hour in class stretches into an hour out of class. What does he see? A stripe—an androgynous looking art student, art student who understands that artists who paint stripes need androgynous looking models? Hasn't he noticed her hourglass shape?

    His house is modern. She has never been in a house this modern, with lines this clean. He offers her an espresso. She could drink it in one glug but sips instead. He says, "Why don't you change? There's a robe in the bathroom."

    She looks at his stripe paintings through a glass wall that separates the living room from the studio. He stands close to her and says, "At least a week into my class I thought you were a male student." He pauses, then says, "I really love how you can pass for a boy."

    She looks back at the studio. Another stripe painting. Was it unfinished? she thinks so. Being a model for an artist who paints stripes will include exposing her hourglass shaped body, which will be very far from being a stripe. She wants to ask him if one model would equal one stripe or if a model could create more stripes by changing her pose, if one model could be enough for a painting with thirty or forty stripes. She doesn't ask. She doesn't want to show her dimensions. If she could have been a stripe she would have.

She looks at herself in the reflection of his glass wall. Holds up her phone and frames her picture. A chart of unfinished stripes ghosts over her curves.

THE SHUDDERING CREAK OF TIME

By Patrick Kruth

The following is based on real events that occurred on the Louth/Monaghan border in the year 1798

I

The barn door opened with the shuddering creak of time. Darkness, a yawning stretch of light. Smell of ripe horse manure and sweet sapless grass. I bent to routine as a thousand mornings before, reaching for the reaping hook. My eyes spied a bloated form propped against a corner bale, trisected by slats of sunlight, splayed out and baring himself.

A bulging stomach protruding over yellowed cotton long Johns, his trousers pooled around his ankles evidencing an abandoned attempt at maintaining decency. Stertorous breathing above in the rafters.

Butchy the Stag, a killer of priests, reliever of heads, a Tory-hunter, lying here now in the condition of Lot and Noah, victim of his own crapulence, vulnerable as I thought he never could be.

The fat handle of a flintlock peaked from the leather belt, its ornate curled hammers cocked, dainty wings on the sandals of Hermes, and it was well I knew them to have delivered many a final message. On his side, a long-curved sabre, sheathed and plainly handled in black.

I raised the reaping hook and mimed three slashes in the air, tracing the strips of sunlight, guides given by God.

It was only two weeks gone, Fr. O'Donovan found unseamed atop a mass stone, dagger in hand, dispatched, the Butchy told the magistrate, while resisting capture.

Unyielding flesh disrupted my practised slices, degenerating to wild flailing hacks. He arose bloodied but was to ground again in the wake of my looming shadow, shackled by his undone trousers and I soon upon him again, his reeking funk disturbed anew by movement and more pungent now as sticky hands scrabbled and pawed. I continued to bring down my hook for long after the spirit had fled.

YOU

You have been seen, Lieutenant Butchy Kirk. You have been watched. But you, too, watch, if only to ensure you are being seen. What good is it to have reached your station and not be noticed? You who are of them, but not one of them. You who saw what they, poor fools, did not. Choosing the winning side is what matters.

You know what it is to lose, you once laboured as them, amongst them. You who broke free of the mire, clipped your accent, bought fitting clothes with your first reward. He gave your mother last rites once, didn't he? Twice provided viaticum.

You are despised. So what? You are despised because secretly they wish they were you. It is only that they are too cowardly. You who shook off superstition and now stop those who would wish to impose it on others. You are somebody.

You... are drunk. Swaying to and fro on your saddle, you grab the beast's sinewy neck to keep from slipping. Nodding, you look into the thickening night. You lean to the side and puke; you are sure they served you bad, emetic grog; they despise you as well. Too Irish, despite all your pretensions. Traitors are hated in all cultures, savage or civilised.

You doze, eased by a steady hoofbeat.

It troubles you, though you'd never admit it aloud. Who is seeing you? Who is watching? That last one, you see him now, so calm, kneeled, orans posture, neck bared, babbling vowels, *et si ambulavero in valle mortis non timebo malum*.

Flashes of hedge lessons *aeternum infernum*. You have regressed again. You had left this magic nonsense behind you. It is no use. The well of your mind has been poisoned.

The road is too open, filled with flowing crowds. You see them all. You had not known you had undone so many. You must not be swept along with them. You must sleep. Smith's barn coalescing from the gloom.

HE

He sat on his heels swirling the dried pool of gore with the tip of an ash twig, transient grooves trailing in its wake, a commander composing a sanguineous battle plan none but he would see.

He arose and stuck an earthen pipe in the left corner of his mouth and drew a match and lit the tobacco. It danced to an instant glow with a soft hiss, and he swiped the stem across his mouth to the right side.

Outside, gathered yeomanry, young Roman faces dressed in the little brief authority afforded by their scarlet uniforms, eager to exercise it in the hope it may hide their glassy essence from both others and themselves.

"A nasty business gentleman, a nasty business indeed. He's to be buried in Inniskeen, Lieutenant, full honours."

"Not the barracks graveyard, Captain?"

"Inniskeen, full honours, and immediately, a coffin is to be fashioned from whatever you can get here."

"Yes, Sir."

He walked through the flurry of moiling men towards the edge of the bog. They were out there now, them all, among the papery birch trees, fleeing retribution long before the alarm was raised.

High pitched squeals of rusted iron nails awoken from long slumber rent from bleached boards. He blew an elongated stream of smoke towards the bog and turned back, making for the barn.

*

He led from the front, marshalling the procession along deserted clay roads hardened by a baking summer sun, twenty men behind taking turns shouldering the coffin, its roughly recycled wood wearing on their shirtless speckled skin. As he went, he watched the hedges and ditches but saw no movement, and not even were there people in the fields and it seemed that even the cattle had retreated to the back pastures.

We

We watched, standing outside McNello's inn in the centre of the village by the junction where the three roads meet. Word had come carried before them and we had been waiting. Men, women, children alike gathered from the fields and mill, hot blood stirring in the midday sun. The children slipped in behind the column, falling into step and adopting expressions of mock solemnity. Forster at their head, full regalia, dew faced, staring straight on, daring us and we whispering and fidgeting, the men hatted and hatted still as the corpse was led past.

Into the pub we men filed. We discussed. We debated. We decided. We planned.

A summer night, darkness sepia-frilled and refusing to close fully. Lingering day past and burgeoning suggestion of day to come. We gathered at the back field behind the graveyard wall on the hill.

We eight climbed the wall and surrounded the freshly mounded grave. We bowed our heads and prayed, begging pardon for the defilement just gone and the defilement to come. We dug, displacing the mound and heaping it thrice over by the grave's edge until the strike of wood and foetid smell of disgorged offal.

Looping ropes underneath, we heaved the coffin up. Dull lolling thuds of the loose meat inside as we carried it atop shoulders to the boundary wall and flung it over, bursting with a splintering crack, ejecting the mangled corpse onto the stony grey soil.

Ye

Ye both stand, arms outstretched over a glowing campfire. A mutual glance suggesting the question ye have asked one another these five weeks now. Five weeks ye come on watch to no reports and come off again with nothing to report. Nothing but the unnerving glare of the locals undoing ye with their eyes, muttering sectarian slurs as they leave loose legged from the Inn. Ye patrol in a pair, never alone. The darkness gathers towards the back end of the graveyard.

Daytime, the women come in dribs and drabs darkly shawled; they pass by soundlessly, tending the graves of relatives. Ye watch them, as they weed and pluck and then move on to spiritual maintenance, garbled intonations and eyes cast aloft, departed souls kept from the licking flames for another day at least.

Thought they paid for such prayers? That was the reason for the split, wasn't it?

None of them stop at his grave, they don't even look.

What does it matter to ye if they dig him up again? Ye knew him for a drunkard and a whoremonger. Disgrace he was let wear the uniform, soiled it in both senses, lowered your standing just by him wearing it, bloody bogger.

One more week and ye can leave. Leave the stag to his papish brethren.

They

They watched and waited. Six weeks to the day after the reburial, the yeomanry gave up their watch and scampered into the night.

They met on the road outside the graveyard, in daylight now, as was not expected. Same process. New coffin. Out through the wrought gates and past the inn, a mock cortège, cheers and yelps and laughs, the coffin surfing the crowd, people eager to place a hand on it, as if it were a holy relic, mothers boosting children aloft to help send it on its way. They six balanced it on the wall of the bridge.

"Throw it in, throw it in," the baying collective cry.

They heave, the roughly hewn wood scraping on the stone as it nosedives for the river, they all surge towards the bridge peering down, seeing it bob before righting itself and surfing down with the current jostled against the banks eventually deciding a steady course, disappearing around the corner to the cheer of the crowd.

They watch long after it is gone, to where they are unsure. Content, however, that it is far away from them.

THE INDICTMENT OF ROBERT FROST

By Kayla King

I recently discovered that Robert Frost is a fucking liar.

This revelation shouldn't have surprised me as it did; after all, graduate school is supposed to be about uprooting our beliefs and finding inspiration in unexpected discoveries. But as I stood at the front of a lecture hall filled with nineteen-year-old under-graduates, their skulls still soft like mushroom caps, all of them looking to me to interpret "The Road Not Taken" with expertise and precision – I didn't feel inspired; I felt duped. Instead of being enlightened, I was incensed.

In response, I've decided to become a traveller who takes the road *more* travelled, the road packed with displeased wanderers and the justifications of their thieving mouths. I'll walk over crunching leaves, listening to their stories, and I'll keep in mind how useless our intentions are – so when I'm in class again, unsteady beneath the weight of my unease, I won't remember their lessons fondly, but with all the bitterness of a student turned teacher, turned fool.

When it comes to meaning, we're all still mildly depressed pre-teens dissecting owl pellets to understand the functionality of regurgitation. It's only after discovering a rat's skull in the palm of our hand that we begin to register the possibility that there are some stories we only tell to make ourselves feel better. All of them, in fact.

*

You fly to Scotland in mid-November to visit your friends.

And [Redacted.]

You're testing the waters, dipping your fingers into [Redacted]'s chest, but finding nothing but sharp rocks and crashing waves.

Should I come back? You ask.

[Redacted] doesn't meet your eyes.

Do you want to?

Do you want me to?

There's no answer, and the rain pours over your heads and between your bodies like a thick, velvet curtain ending the scene. Except when you go to walk away, turn your back and leave [Redacted] standing alone centre stage, he's there again, reaching between raindrops and pulling you back into the whirlpool around his ribs, and when his mouth is on yours again, and his hands are in your hair, it doesn't seem to matter anymore that *no* answer is an answer.

You return to Scotland for another semester abroad because you miss your friends – or because you're stupid.

You know things are different when you have to buy your own gin and tonic, to maim and disembowel your own lime. You know things are different when he touches the back of your chair instead of your shoulder, the table instead of your hand. You know things are different when he says he's glad things aren't awkward, glad that you can be friends.

You know things are different when you meet the girl he hooked up with after you left.

In retaliation, you hook up with the boy from Ireland who asks if he can lick your eyes. He's tall and doesn't play guitar, which is enough deviation from [Redacted] that attraction comes easily. You spend twelve weeks alternating between the highs and lows of rebounding, and when you finally go home in late spring, you're exhausted, every drop of tenderness inside of you wrung out through the cracks in your chest. You hug your mother upon arrival, and later, when she asks if you regret it, you say no, that it's better you know for sure he didn't want you.

*

Stunned and angry as I may be with Mr. Frost, I kind of understand the temptation to let our early decisions cast long, dignified shadows on the rest of our lives. Because we don't often get to choose between paths that are clear and clean and paths that are jungled – mostly, it's a slogging run between piles of shit in either direction. And now I'm thinking about the relevance of poetry and how – by the estimation of someone smarter than me, or at least with a smarter voice – there is no path by which our stories derive deeper meaning. We are bereft, telling each other lies about the hows and the whys because it makes the taste of helplessness less rancid.

*

You don't want to stay in Louisville. You're bored of your job in healthcare, where you're steadily climbing the corporate ladder, making more money than you ever have before. You're bored of the rapidly drying dating pool. Bored of the famous Kentucky bourbon and mint juleps, both of which taste rotten. You're bored of spending every day surrounded by nurses, doctors, technicians, and medical assistants, bored of the feeling that you're the only one who hasn't figured everything out. Trying to talk to your co-workers makes your lungs feel bruised; they hear your stories like mountains hear the fields of gravel hundreds of miles below.

The thing is, you get bored everywhere. Five years is your limit. Five years and you're itching, ready to fling off your skin and slide to the ground in your new form – an earthworm, perhaps, or a slug.

Your parents are conveniently planning a move to Texas at the time – San Antonio specifically, which seems like an excellent place for rebirth. But, then again, you believed that about Whitewater too. And Boise. And Louisville. Why should this be different? How can you justify upsetting your life – again – when you're almost thirty? When you have a 401K and a goddamn gym membership that sometimes you use?

So, you google it. You google San Antonio, Dallas, Houston, and Austin, and somewhere down the rabbit hole, you end up in San Marcos, eye-to-eye with Texas State University.

Here's the thing. Here's the secret. You've been telling people since you graduated with your Bachelor's Degree (almost ten years ago) that you would get an MFA. Someday, you said. When I'm ready, you said. But you never actually planned on getting one. It's one of those things you said to your parents, your grandparents, and sometimes yourself. Red tape gives you anxiety; applications and letters of recommendation and the GRE dry your enthusiasm into a wrinkled ball that gets blown away by your hot air.

But Texas State doesn't require the GRE, and you only need letters of recommendation if you plan to be an IA, which is something you're still too scared to admit you want. So, you make a deal with yourself. You'll move to Texas, but only if you apply to Texas State. You need a reason to move again, and this time, it better be a damn good one.

*

Our paths are dirty, overgrown with spines and poison ivy; they make us itch, and they make us bleed. The scenery can be a lovely distraction, though, provided we're willing to change course at any given moment to capture what's always just out of reach. Each winding road we follow is littered with diversions, off-shoots, and distractions in every direction, and the cherry blossoms seem sweet, drifting in the air around us – until we have the tiny pink corpses of broken hearts getting caught in our hair. What we want isn't always what we need, and sometimes what we need is to cut open our palms and leave a trail of blood on the path for those behind us to follow.

*

You write in your journal the following entries over the course of six months:

"I've resigned myself to the fact that I won't get accepted. I'll suck it up and submit an application, just so I know the process. I'm only applying to one school this time – maybe more next year. We'll see."

"I have to get this application done. I can't stress about it anymore."

"Still haven't finished the application – just another thing I'm worried about. Feeling helpless and stuck again."

"All the technical stuff is done – now I just have to finish the damn stories."

"Application. Submitted. Feels good to say that. Still certain I won't get in, but at least now I know what the process is like."

When you get your acceptance phone call on March 6, 2020, your journal entry reads like this:

"I got into grad school. Surreal and unbelievable, and all I can think is… now what?"

*

Choices are not significant in the way I always thought. Would our decisions mean more if they were always difficult? Less, if they were always easy? No – I'll walk where I'll walk, and I'll do it, not because it's right, or easy, or complex, or will make my life more meaningful in the end. I'll do it because I have to – because there's no choice at all except to live or lay down and die.

*

The first man you date in Texas is – of course – a fucking nurse. You spend the week before your first date wishing he did anything else. You've had your fill of the medical life. When he tells you stories, you remember things you're in therapy to forget – the little girl with semen in her urine who you carried through the clinic because she had escaped her aunt's clutches and was running for the door, her tiny fist a rock against your heart; the mother who checked her ten-year-old son in for a twisted ankle before walking out back behind the clinic and sticking a needle in her arm; the man with kidney failure who died in the parking lot as he was coming in for an appointment – you watched your colleagues delivering CPR to his pale, swollen body only because his nephew was watching and not because they believed they could save him. He was already dead.

You don't want to date a nurse, and even though he's charming and attractive, and he invites you to his birthday party after your very first date, and you go, and it's kind of fun, kind of a disaster (your golf swing is fucking embarrassing), your heart is only half in it. The two of you end up mutually ghosting each other – your texts petering out to pleasantries until they finally, mercifully, stop.

*

Now that I've had time to reconsider, I am less angry with Robert Frost for his subtle deception – because the biggest liar has always been me. Every day I feel myself ticking towards old age and old talent and wonder how many paths would have bypassed this stagnant middle. Which bad things could I have avoided? Which good things may I have missed? It's all the same, though, in the end. Meaning immersed in mud or meaning immersed in shit.

It's not a matter of which path is right or wrong – it's a matter of what I will say thirty, forty, or fifty years from now with a sigh and a sad, strained smile.

*

The things you like are seldom good for you; things like red velvet cake and sex and lime-twisted gin and writing. They fill your head with the sounds of the ocean and bring your heart one beat closer to popping open and filling your chest with blood. You're chasing indulgences, no matter which paths they lead you down, and you're never going to stop because it feels too fucking good, and there's nothing and no one to hold you back. You've made damn sure of that, haven't you? (Glutton. Hedonist. Slut. Liar. When you end up famous for your best-told disaster, don't say me and Robert Frost didn't warn you.)

*

I don't tell my under-grads I only figured out the meaning behind "The Road Not Taken" the night before our lecture or that I have been reading it wrong since the seventh grade. I don't tell them I'm a liar who is constantly honing my craft, a mediocre student masquerading as a teacher. I don't tell them I enjoy binge-watching Korean dramas more than I like reading any of the assigned texts for our class, or that I live in perpetual fear of unsolicited questions.

I could tell them if they pressed me – that failure is inescapable and judgements fickle – that there is no right or wrong when you're buried chest-deep in quicksand, struggling to breathe. That academia is just another pocket to put losers like me who the real world spat back out.

That sometimes things in life are just hard because they're hard, and there's no value in agony.

But that's not what they're in college to hear. Right now, they want the lies – the idealistic adages about self-fulfilment and non-conformity. They want me to stand on my pedestal and tell them how meaningful their paths are, how rewarding and gratifying it is to trudge, barefoot, up the rocky hillside of their own ambitions until they finally reach the top, bleeding but alive. Most of them would like to hear that the suffering is worth it – that it's the difference between someone who *wanted* to succeed and the one who *did* – and I don't have the intestinal fortitude to mess that up for them.

So, I'll smile and say that I have no regrets – that my path may have been long and caked with mud, but it got me here, to the front of this lecture hall. And that, I'll tell them, has made all the difference.

A CLOVEN HOOF

By Sam Martone

On the drive out to the stables, we pass billboards advertising Mysterious Thing. A tourist trap, although I'm not sure how many tourists pass through here.

Only ten miles until Mysterious Thing!

The typeface drips like slime, a font of dread.

"What if it's a swamp monster," Byron says, eyes on endless road ahead.

"No swamps around here," I say.

"Mysterious, right?"

We love the billboards. We joke about Mysterious Thing, speculate about its nature, is it wild or tame, is it alive or dead, can you feed it.

What is it? What is it?!? Mysterious Thing awaits you – three miles!

There's an undercurrent between us. We both know it, but nothing's happened yet. We've been friends for so long, and he's seeing other people, so it doesn't feel real. It's not real, yet, but something is bubbling. He'd be thrilled to know how desire paws around inside me, how badly I want him, like a TV show sex scene, no foreplay, just bucking, bed-breaking. But he can't understand what else I want: for it to be singular, the only thing he wants.

Last chance for a harrowing glimpse at Mysterious Thing!

We pass the exit, the shack where Mysterious Thing rests. We both agree, some things are better left a mystery, though we don't always agree which things. On the opposite side of the road, there's an identical set of billboards for drivers coming the other direction. We only see blank wooden backs.

*

We go out to the stables to watch the horses. Our friend Mercedes used to take riding lessons here. We still come because it's one of the biggest stables in the state, and it's far enough from the city that it feels like a getaway when we don't have time for a real one. Normally, I'm content to migrate from my climate-controlled living room to my climate-controlled office and back again, put on reruns or a movie I missed when it was in theatres. But Byron's desire to go, go, go is infectious. Even though I hate how the heat sticks to me, I can't decline his invitations or deny the way something in me shifts when I'm with him—from easily irritable and burnt out to curious and calm and hungry for more.

We sit on folding chairs, the splayed-out fabric kind you bring camping or to kids' soccer games. With only short wooden fences separating them from vast desert, the riderless horses look almost wild against the horizon. They kick up dirt behind them like the yellow clouds we see covering Phoenix on the news, dust storms we can't see when we're in the hot heart of them. We watch and talk for hours, until the spreading neon marmalade of sunset cuts sharp outlines into the horses' sinewy muscles. The light hits Byron's forearms the same way.

"There's something sexual about them," Byron says, but Byron sees something sexual in everything.

"No," I say. "There's not."

Byron describes his attraction like a compass, pointing clearly in one direction, toward one person, but frequently disrupted by the magnetic fields of others. He's been trying on new identities since his long-time girlfriend broke up with him: bisexual, polyamorous. Nothing quite fits, so he casts one off and searches for the next. Recently, he landed on pansexual.

"It means I like everyone. Or could," Byron explained when he told me, even though I didn't ask. "Comes from Pan—the Greek god, because he's a little bit of everything."

"That's not where it comes from."

"It is," he insisted. Our group of friends, we call Byron twenty percent, because twenty percent of the time, he isn't telling the truth. He tells you something straight-faced, a funny anecdote or tidbit of trivia, only to break as soon as you react: *Yeah, not really, I just made that up.*

"Wasn't Pan half-man, half-goat?" I said, playing along.

"No, no. He had a snake for a tail. Shoulders of a tiger. Cow stomachs."

"Twenty percent," I said, and Byron laughed. Now, I look at Byron and imagine the ensemble of lovers in his life as disparate animal parts. Head of a lion. Wings of a bat. I wonder, if he were to add me to his chimera, what I'd be.

"What are their hooves called?" I say.

"The horses?"

"You know, like deer or sheep have cloven hooves. What are horse hooves?"

"I don't know. Horse hooves?"

Night soaks the sky. Soon the horses will disappear in the dark, just heavy clops and snorts, monsters of shadow and sound. Stable hands start ushering them into their pens. Mercedes told me *grooms* was the preferred term for stable hands, after I asked her if she'd ever hooked up with any of them. *Married to their animals*, she joked.

"Did you know," Byron says, "that once, horses had three toes, and over time they fused into one?"

"Twenty percent?" I say, but he might be telling the truth. He's still peering through the dark at the animals, their forms blending amorphously with the grooms, silhouettes of failed centaurs.

*

On the drive back, Byron tells me he slept with Mercedes last weekend.

"Oh, shit," I say.

"It's not serious."

"Does she know that?"

"Come on, she insisted."

He wants me to ask more questions, but I won't. I've never met anyone like Byron. He dutifully reports on the other people he's seeing, what arguments they're having. He points out places they've had sex. He thinks this honesty brings us closer. "I don't want to hide any part of me," he told me once, but I think he hopes this will absolve him of any wrongdoing, prevent my feelings from getting hurt.

Telling me about Mercedes transmutes the stables into just another landmark on his map of liaisons. I imagine them outside the horse stalls, rolling on a bale of hay, even though they weren't there. They were at his place, he tells me, in his room. I was across town, watching television, thinking about Byron.

"What if Mysterious Thing is just a horse," he says. "The guy who runs the place doesn't get out much, he's never seen anything like it."

I don't join in.

He tries again. "What if it's the corpse of a ghost?"

He wants me to say *ghosts don't have corpses*. He wants to reply *mysterious, right?*

We pass another billboard, and another, promising the fright of our lives, the anomaly of the century. I'm looking out into the deep dark of the desert, to see what might roam there, uncaptured. I'm trying to ignore the transparent reflection in my window of Byron in the driver's seat, the way the tendons in his leg tense as he presses the gas or switches to brake. But then Byron puts on his turn signal, takes the off-ramp.

"I thought it was better left a mystery," I say.

"Maybe not."

*

Inside, we pay a bored woman behind the booth our ten-dollar entry fee. She jerks her thumb, and we walk down a hallway that smells of sawdust and mildew. It leads us to a dim room with a wooden display case elevated on a platform.

We walk up the creaky platform steps, slowly, as though not wanting to wake anything. At the top of the steps, the point of no return, I almost grab Byron's hand. But I don't. I don't want to fabricate another moment we'll pretend didn't happen. We approach the case and look down, past the thumbprints smudged across the glass, into the open, haunted eyes of Mysterious Thing.

It's the carcass of something indescribable, large but withered, hideously beautiful. Something I've never seen, something I'll never forget, its hooves not cloven or horse, but a third, unknowable, kind. As we stare down at the thing, gnarled in its bed of dry colourless hay, I have a memory of Byron on top of me, inside me, our fevered rutting, and I understand that, somehow, it's already happened, and also that it never will.

"Oh, come on," Byron says. "I know what that is." I almost, for one thrilling moment, believe him.

CARTOGRAPHY

By Aisling Cahill

The basement again. Floor minus two, announced by a mechanical voice with a generic English accent. The doors ping open. You're here to find out which body parts are pushing against which other body parts, looking for somewhere else to go. The porter is gone, abandoning your wheelchair, leaving you almost in the way.

'Lovely day', he'd insisted, his accent echoing against the walls.

And you'd nodded, afraid to do much more, in case everything inside of you would brim up and spill over; a soft, slow fizz. Your room doesn't have a window. There's been no daylight in days.

You're told the surgery went well, but everything feels strange. Awkward and swollen, like you're much too large, bursting from the back of your hospital gown. The physio took a photo so that you could see. Your back's an imitation Picasso, blue lines drawn across your transparent skin, a map so they could find where they needed to cut you open. X marks the spot. The dressing a spongy white rectangle, stained with blood in a shape that resembles Brazil. You wonder now if you'll ever get there, or anywhere. If you'll ever move with ease again.

You check your ticket twice, forgetting your number straight away. A nurse handed it to you, so that you could keep your place in line. As though you were simply queueing for the bank.

You're not supposed to sit, or bend or lift anything for the next three months. You'd wondered how you'd manage it, if you'd cross the days off your calendar in frustration, but now you understand. It'll be months of lying in bed, afraid to move, worried about the ways the big wide world can hurt you. You used to be invincible. Now, you can just about feel your legs. Your left foot is missing still. They said it'd take time. Nerves are slow to regenerate. You imagine your insides stitching themselves back to life, growing like the roots of a tree. Everything fresh and green, an internal Spring coinciding with the month of May.

Another MRI, on your spine again, but this time a different part. You were taught to count the vertebrae. Stepping stairs to your brain. So many of them slipping out of place, the path muddled, the pain a constant. You think about how everything hurts, but at least it hasn't found your elbows. Little victories.

A ticket number is called, and that same nurse reappears, asking if you can walk. You shrug and nod at the same time. There's a difference between can and should. She wheels you from a waiting room filled with men who wouldn't make eye contact to this room with the big machine, the largest magnet you've ever seen.

A man appears from behind the window, asking your name, but never surrenders his. The table's lowered as far as it'll go. Your gown has opened at the back, and you pull yourself away from the chair, timid as a child, the noise of your sweaty skin slowly peeling from the plastic. The only human sound in the room. You prop yourself up, but your legs won't lift. You tell them, the nurse, and the anonymous man, and without asking, they bend, grabbing a useless leg each and lifting you so that you're up, lying flat on your back. The roar that escapes your throat belongs to somebody else because you don't complain. You take it, every time, without so much as a whimper. They ignore it, propping headphones over your ears, instructing you to be still. A manual on how to be the perfect patient. You don't hear them leave the room.

The table moves into the machine, eating you whole. You know it'll spit you out in twenty minutes. It does little to still your frenzied heart.

Somebody else's tears run into your ears, and you let them. You're not allowed to move. The unkindness of medicine when you're complicated. It's been years since somebody's said that it'll be okay. You were once a tourist moving across the land of the sick, but you've lived here now for longer than you care to admit.

The ticket's still clutched in your hand.

24 FLASH FICTION

WAR MAKER

By E J DELANEY

My name is the trigger.

"Boulos," she says, putting the r-sound in the middle and ending with *liss* rather than *loss*. "Boulos Asali."

Resentment surges through me.

It's not that she gets my name wrong, quite the opposite. Where the other kids have hammers for tongues, Taliah Bates-Blue keeps the vowels soft. But she's the school captain. Her pronunciation is so deliberate, so precise. Even in getting it right she's mocking me, pulling me up for my uncompromising stance when we were first introduced.

"Why aren't you in costume?" She's cornered me just inside the school gates, blocking my path as Yaḥyā runs off to join his classmates on the oval. "It's multicultural day. You should be celebrating!"

What's to celebrate?

I look over at Yaḥyā. Despite the heat, my little brother is happily showing off his black and red embroidered vest and his round, patterned hat with its funny tassel. Even at nine o'clock in the morning I can feel the sun lording it overhead; it hangs oppressive, its touch drawing out sweat from beneath my collar. Brisbane in December? It's too hot to be dressing up.

Besides, nobody *really* wants us to be Syrian. We're Australian now, right? Isn't that the point?

"Oh, but you've got the colours." Taliah raises her chin at the stripes on my shirt. "Red, black and white, right? That's good. I'm glad you're joining in."

I'm *not* joining in; I'm opting out. I ask:

"What about you?" Usually I only see her in school uniform, but today she's wearing dusty brown boots, blue jeans, and a button-up shirt not unlike mine. She has an oversized hat placed loosely on her head, a few strands of long blonde hair trailing from its stiff leather brim. "Where are *you* supposed to be from?"

Taliah reaches up to touch the hat.

"It's an Akubra," she explains. "My grandad's. We're from out west originally. Kaimkillenbun, just past Dalby." She must see that I don't understand. "Cattle country."

I shake my head.

"I guess I don't have any of this." Taliah turns slightly, directing me to the stalls set up on the oval—the impromptu bazaar with its brightly coloured Indian totas and Chinese lanterns and Greek garlands and all the other touches from a hundred different cultures. "I'm not Aboriginal and I didn't want to wear one of those yellow and green clown wigs like the Fanatics." She cringes at the thought. "It's like what Miss Fasham said: without the diversity we're kind of bland."

Our music teacher—Mr Watego—walks past carrying an armful of dot-patterned digeridoos. Reece King trails behind him. Reece is Taliah's former co-captain, a red-headed Aussie with fair skin and freckles. He glares sideways as he trudges past. "Taliah," he mutters. "Novak."

He's likening me to Novak Djokovic (who shares my haircut but is Serbian, not Syrian). I glare at him.

"You don't seem happy, Boulos." Taliah either ignores our hostility or isn't aware of it.

Didn't she see us fighting last week? Didn't she stand there, yelling at us to stop, while we rolled about on the grass, grappling and throwing punches at each other?

I can still hear her voice, as clear in my mind as the woman on the radio. There'd been another car bomb back home in Jaramana. Twelve dead, forty-three wounded. The TV news had shown white ribbons hanging from the balconies, and black and white death notices glued to the walls.

Can't she see, it's all part of the same conflict?

Happy? Of course I'm not happy.

What's to be happy about?

*

It's exactly three years since the war started for me, a notch in time that allows even for Brisbane being seven hours ahead of Damascus. I remember those first seconds: waking to the rhythmic pulse of helicopter blades; the whistle of artillery shells in the darkness outside. Each thump sounds dull, almost far away. But the shudder of the floor is close. There's a hot flash of orange through the window.

For a long moment I'm alone. My other senses shut down and I'm left with smell—the sour, pungent scent of exploded shells mixing with the sweet fragrance of jasmine.

Then everything else rushes back and *Yaḥyā* is beside me, clinging to me, moaning in terror. Our parents are there too, hugging us both and murmuring prayers. I'll never know who was firing at whom—which faction of the government or the rebels or the many groups who support or oppose them—but that's when it happens.

Another shell explodes, closer than any of the others. The whole building moves!

The floor tilts, juddering sideways and down. Shrieking, we fall back, swallowed up by the dying apartment block. I crash into the wall by the door, hurting my shoulder. My face burns with tears. I hear a tiny, hot voice I barely recognise as my own crying out, "We have to fight! We have to fight them!"

At dawn the next day we venture outside. The sun itself seems hesitant, poking its rays past half-collapsed buildings onto streets strewn with wreckage; onto people shuffling, some crying, some dazed. We're alive. The realisation brings trembling relief. *We're alive!*

But the city-suburb of Jaramana isn't. Our neighbourhood has turned overnight into a burnt-out, half-standing ruin. The civil war has come, and neither concrete nor brick can withstand it. I see a van smoking in the aftermath, fire still licking at its jolly blue paintwork. I see a mangled bike just like my own lying twisted and dead on the road. Our apartment block—our home—sags out over the street as if shot in the stomach.

I look to my father. I expect to see rage—the same rage that burns in me—but instead he seems... resigned. No, not resigned. *Determined*. But grim and sad, too. He touches my mother's shoulder, comforting her even as she murmurs reassurances to *Yaḥyā*.

Why isn't papa angry? Doesn't he want to lash out at whoever did this?

The answer is no. Papa has a different fight in mind—the fight to escape.

That morning, we gather what we can carry and walk the train tracks to Lebanon. Men herd us together with other refugees and put us in a camp; in a box with canvas walls and a rusty screen door. There is one toilet outside, and one water tank, shared by everyone. We wash, when possible, in buckets of cold water.

We mostly stay dirty.

There's no school for *Yaḥyā* and me. The locals don't want us here, and mama says not to blame them; that the people of Lebanon have their own problems. So, we huddle in our box, and she teaches us what she can.

Papa looks for work. He leaves early each morning and comes home late. Nine months pass with nothing to show, then he backs in through the screen door one evening, he and another man carrying a heater between them. Papa looks happy as Ghawwar al-Toshe; even happier a month later when he finds kerosene to run it.

The cockroaches love us. They're drawn to our box now, and I wake at night to find one scuttling up and down my chest. Scorpions come inside, too. *Yaḥyā* gets up too sleepy and forgets to check, almost stepping on one.

This is our new life.

"Not forever," papa tells us. He squeezes mama's hand and turns tired eyes to the canvas ceiling. "There will be better times, better places."

He spends twenty-nine months wrestling the embassy in Beirut. Two and a half years since we left Jaramana! There are no Christmases in our box: a small dead tree, yes, but no decorations hanging from it; no Papa Noel in costume and beard, bringing presents by horseback. *Yaḥyā* and I grow slowly out of our clothes.

Everything is grey.

And then, in a rush, it all changes again. We find ourselves at the airport, the four of us with our three battered suitcases. From Beirut to Qatar and then on to Brisbane, with its warm Australian winters and hot, humid summers and nothing in between except sudden bouts of heavy rain.

It doesn't seem real. I'm here but I'm not.

"*Katkoot*," mama whispers to *Yaḥyā* as the plane touches down; and to me: "*Asfoor*. We made it. It is over."

She sighs, the tension dropping at last from her shoulders. But she's wrong; it's not over.

Not for me.

*

"I've only ever seen you smile once," Taliah Bates-Blue says. "You scored a goal in soccer and—"

I remember. Back home I used to play football—all the neighbourhood kids did—so when Miss Fasham led us out onto the oval, some part of me came alive. I darted past a defender and struck, my shot embedding itself deep in the top left corner. Goal! My teammates cheered. A couple of the boys came up and gave me high-fives. For one dazed, blissful moment, the war slipped from my thoughts.

The news that night brought it crashing back: helicopters over Jaramana, barrel bombs dropping like TNT coconuts, nine dead, countless wounded.

Ceasefire or no, I haven't played football since.

"... but your brother smiles all the time," Taliah is saying. "And it's such a *nice* smile." She shakes her head again. "I don't get it."

I look to where *Yaḥyā* is parading about in the sunshine, showing off his costume some more and the *kibbeh labanīyah* he helped mama make last night.

"Ee," I grunt; meaning *yes*, I don't get it either.

*Yaḥ*yā seems not to notice the war. He actually likes it that his classmates reverse the vowel sounds of his name, turning *Yah*-here into *Yee*-ha! He takes it as acceptance and reciprocates by very solemnly saying 'G'day' to everyone he meets, even though that's old slang that none of the Aussie kids use.

I love my brother. I'm glad *Yaḥ*yā is happy. But even so...

"What have you brought there?" Taliah asks. She nods at the plastic container I have tucked under my arm.

"*Baklava*."

"Are you going to offer me some?"

I peel the lid back, revealing the sweet diamond-shaped pastries that are papa's contribution to the Asali cooking legacy.

Taliah leans forward. Her hat casts too much of a shadow, so she takes it off, releasing cascades of the sun-yellow hair I still find so strange.

"They look a bit like baklava," she says, using the Greek pronunciation.

"Same thing. Ours are better though."

"Mmm! And what about your brother? Did he bring something?"

"*Kibbeh labanīyah*. Minced lamb balls with yoghurt."

"Lamb! Very Australian."

"Very Syrian."

"Well, it sure beats damper. Half the *school* has made damper."

"Damper?"

"It's a kind of bread." Taliah wrinkles her nose. "Stockmen ate it to survive in the outback. It probably tastes okay if you're really hungry."

"Bread?" I consider this. I think of mama draping flattened dough over the *saj*; peeling it off and slapping it in circles from hand to hand. I remember *Yaḥḥyā* trying it back in Jaramana and making a giggling mess. "And that's the national dish here?"

"Like I said, we're a bit bland."

We stand awhile, not saying anything. The school oval lies before us, alive with colour and sound: Vietnamese pinwheel fans; Sudanese girls in bedazzling *thobes*; Jamaicans boys playing hand drums while Mr McCormick, the deputy principal, tries to blow Advance Australia Fair on the bagpipes.

Compared to the blackened grey rubble of the war, the bereaved wailing of wives and mothers, none of this makes sense. It's not real; it isn't survival.

But maybe—

The notion creeps in, catching me off-guard. *Maybe it's what comes after?*

Just then Reece King traipses past for a second time.

"Boo," the redhead scowls. His eyes seem to burn, and the words smoulder under his breath. "*Boo*, and get *lost*."

My own lips twist into a sneer, but as Reece mooches off back towards the music room, I suddenly feel more sad than angry.

"You know..." Taliah begins.

"What?"

"Well—" She hesitates, then plunges on: "I was just wondering if you realise, he's not being mean to you because you're from Syria."

I shake my head, not following. Taliah continues:

"It's because I talk to you, I think."

"But why should—?"

"In *Australia*, Boulos, we have this thing called being jealous."

She says 'Australia' as if that's the foreign word. My name still sounds like she's practised it very carefully in front of a mirror, but it's not so mocking in comparison.

Still, my eyebrows hunch together. Reece King, jealous of me? But why—?

"Coming?" Taliah asks.

She pushes away from the fence and starts off towards the bazaar. I look to the multi-coloured tents and the crazy bustle of cultures, and I find myself stepping after her.

"This— this hat from your grandpa," I ask. "Why do you call it a cobra?"

"*Akubra.*" Taliah smiles back over her shoulder. "People think it's an Aboriginal word, but actually we don't really know where it comes from. It's just part of our history now."

Her cheeks dimple, and for the second time in three years my world tilts—without explosions this time, dizzying in the bright Australian sunshine.

Because there's nothing cruel in Taliah's speech. There's nothing grey or cold about her. She's just here, and so am I; and she's smiling at *me*.

"Boulos Asali," she proposes.

My name is still a trigger, but her voice is soft, and the only conflict right now is between lamb and damper. Taliah says she wants to meet *Yaḥyā*, and to try *Kibbeh labanīyah*. We head out onto the oval, where I choke on a rock-hard lump of Australian bread. The war has shifted theatre.

"Not bad," I tell her. She stares at me in disbelief, and I swallow the mouthful before clarifying: "It's *awful*. I like your hat, Taliah Bates-Blue, but this is the worst bread ever."

They're the sort of words I could have spat, but they surprise me by coming out without rancour; as if I'm back home or joking with *Yaḥyā*. They surprise Taliah, too.

She claps her hands once, drawing them to her chest. Something in her expression brings back memories of the *dabke* dancers at my auntie's wedding. War or no war, she looks to the sky and laughs.

All at once, the thrumming in my ears sounds nothing like helicopter blades.

WAR MAKER

DARK HOURS

By Ian Ledward

Beauty and the Beast

He could barely stand, had not eaten for over a day, yet still felt the cold shivering waves of nausea spiralling in doppler spasms, threatening to burst his head and spill the contents of his gut. All he wanted to do was lie down and sleep but the flashing lights and beeps, unable to decide what to do with themselves, just kept coming. A soft, thick darkness soon won this tug of war, its shadows draping themselves across his fading comprehension, closing everything as he fell.

He could hear voices, partly shouted, partly spoken, real or imagined, coming from far away and sounding like spoons rattling in a drawer.

"Shut that fucking door."

"Not very polite," came the appeasing sing-song response.

"Oh. Excuse me. Will you please shut that fucking door?"

"Spoken like a true gentleman from The Ferry," said the woman in a light-hearted tone in answer to the voice that was thin, sharp, and repetitive like a bit-part actor rehearsing lines. *Was that me*, he wondered, *did I say that?* And as the whirlpool of nausea began pulling him down again, he imagined the original owner of the tirade as a sparse, balding scarecrow who could easily have fit into a cardboard box. Together, the words had a certain cachet though. *Shut that fucking door. Come here will ye? Where the fuck d'ye think yer going?* They had pedigree, well-worn with frequent usage and not designed for conversation but as a command, directed towards someone mute and subservient. Try them out but be careful where. Maybe under a railway bridge when the train is going over but remember, they do have to be shouted, even screamed for best effect.

In his drug-induced fevered state he was trying to pull back the trailing threads of a departing dream. Time was moving backwards and forwards precipitating in a pendulum of places, faces, and events. Then there was the sweet odour of rancid honey. He vomited, without realising he was out of control.

She was a princess, a goddess even, and he was totally in her power but within that there was a deep warmth of comfort. She was dressed all in blue and her face shimmered. He lay all but naked on a bed. Was she asking him something? Her voice was deep and throaty, but she had a softness about her.

"Have you ever done this before? Just relax," she was saying. Everything was fuzzy and he was thinking, *don't know... can't remember*, but just couldn't speak the words.

'Wha...? Naw?' was all he managed in a stretched-out groan, thinking, *Is it like Chinese beads?* He felt he was trying to crawl from a maze of mirrors reflecting endless confused repetitions of his thoughts.

He read laughter in her faraway musical voice as she rolled his cock between her palms. Her hair was a dark, streaked blond and was pinned in a bundle with what seemed like pink cosmos flowers tucked in the side. As she gently teased him, he tried to get into a more active position, but she was having none of it and gently pushed him down.

"I'm Cathy, by the way."

Hello Catheter. Thoughts but not words.

"What's your date of birth?"

"Aaw." *Date of birth? Fire Dog, Chinese beads, opium*, still only thinking, *what have they given me?*

"Don't worry, just relax and leave it all to me." The voice was calm and reassuring.

What? OK. Don't stop for me. He was trying to say, but all she heard was something like, "Whah, whah, dawh, awh..."

"Did you feel that?"

"Mmm..." *Bit funny*... he was thinking.

"Did that hurt?"

"Nnnn? Mmm?" Only groans and mumbles. *Felt funny*. Then, suddenly words, "Ask Alice, she'll know."

"Is that your wife?"

"Ugh?"

"Can you cough?"

"Mmm?"

DARK HOURS

"Cough?" He coughed.

"Is that better?"

Better? "Mmm," and feeling the wonderful surge of release all through his loins.

As she bent closer over his midriff, his passing thought, *What's she...is she going to...? No, not with a mask on, but nice thought, later maybe, nice hair.*

"Just you relax now." Abandoning himself to her gentle, expert hands he watched pink flowers fall across the bed as he drifted back into second-hand reality.

Kings and Queens of the Night

He was listening out for their coming. The Kings and Queens of the night. What strange, soft tonal poetry they make as they prowl the corridors in the dark hours before dawn, their little tote bags on their backs. The King, whose bite does not sting and she, the Queen, who is quick and clean, and tonight, he was one of her anointed as he lay helpless, defenceless, floating and thinking, *Here, there, everywhere and nowhere baby.*

"You have been chosen," she seemed to be saying to him. "It is your turn."

She came at him with her single tooth, her extensible tubular organ. A gloomy situation was becoming even darker.

"If you relax, I will not hurt you." And even though he could only see her hazel eyes and brown hair, he knew there was an undeniable power and strength of will in her as he extended his arm in an offering of peace, of resigned acceptance.

Quick and clean. Quick and clean. He repeated his mantra as that single steel fang entered his body and he felt a nervous tingle through his fingers and toes.

"It will be over soon and then you can sleep."

Sleep, he thought, *oh, real sleep. Yeah, that's what I want.* But when it came, his half dreams were the fever-dreams of childhood illness. Colours with unrecognisable tastes and shapes that had curdling smells, sounds that were like rough sacking at the back of his throat and things that moved, twisting, and coiling in the air like jagged spirals of soft barbed wire that snagged at tastes just beyond his grasp.

"Here, take these and sleep well, and if you can't sleep well, just you sleep as well as you can." Standing for a few moments to watch him, the Queen's voice was different now and sounded far away.

The Night of the Blood-Sucker

"What time is it?" He woke from a shallow sleep. The sudden brightness of light from a head torch made his gut heave. The wall clock indicated 3.00am, the classic hour the Gestapo would knock on the doors of the fearful half-expectant, catching them at their most vulnerable.

"Time for blood," she whispered.

"Aw no… I was dreaming," he replied, what shallow sleep there had been, stolen. All his doubts and fears waking again, boxing for a corner in his thumping head. The rubber strap tightened, a gentle slap, then a sharp pain in the crook of his elbow. His right knee jerked reflexively, hitting the arm of his assailant. The spike she was holding drove deeper into his arm.

"Aaaggh!" Was it his pain or the pain of another self? Did either qualify as a cogency?

"Sorry! We'll need to do it again." *We? No*…. he thought, wondering if the needle had broken off. She trembled but managed it on the third go. Everything seemed far away, through a telescope the wrong way round with the sound of an old gramophone record playing, 'Ring a ring o' roses', slowing and slurring and suddenly coming to a halt.

The Return of the King

A sensation slurred. A subtle change in the air, a rustle of fabric. Had he been dreaming? Had he actually slept? A shadow stood by the side of his bed looking down at him. Startled, he asked, "How long have you been there?" feeling that sense of unease when he realised someone had been watching him.

"A minute, maybe." A large man with short blond, spiky hair stood looking at him. He exuded a strength that seemed strangely at odds with his voice which had a soft, hypnotic quality to it as he replied, "They called me. Can I look at it again?" Taking the arm gently in his large hands. "What happened?"

"Don't know. Doesn't feel right."

"See the way the gauze on your arm is damp from the fluid. Something's torn loose."

"Oh." Thoughts of those movies where Arnie Schwarzenegger jumps out of his hospital bed, fit as a fiddle, pulls out all those trailing tubes and hanging bags of fluid from bulging muscles, scattering them everywhere and runs out the door, calling all the odds, and goes off to knock shit out of the bad guys.

"The cannula has tissued."

"Doesn't sound good."

"We need to sort this out." *Another we. Another needle, something sharp again.* His nausea increased.

"Don't clench your fist! It's the worst thing you can do." Probably the nearest the King's mellifluous whisper ever approached a shout yet it still had the urgency of command.

The king does not sting, he was thinking, and in the next moment the King was done and gone.

Good, Bad and Downright Ugly News

It was as if a gathering of directionless light had been hovering and swarming in the corridor and, no longer able to contain itself, came bursting into the places where darkness had been lurking.

"What time is it?"

"Nearly midnight," she replied.

"Thought it was morning."

"I'd be away home if it was."

"Why's it so bright?"

"Sorry, need the lights to see what I'm doing." She had a voice that let him see the smile behind her mask and as his eyes adjusted, he saw a twinkle in hers as she poked a lock of hair behind her ear. *Blood again,* he thought as his eyelids felt as though they were smeared with treacle. Hospital staff are obsessed by keeping lights on and doors open and even prisoners on remand have more rights including the privacy of a locked door. *Did I agree to their terms and conditions?* He wondered, then asked, "Where are your flowers?"

Ignoring this she asked, "Would you like the good news or the bad news first?" She warbled.

There's never a right answer to this, he thought, but he wasn't given the time to ponder.

"Your oxygen level is maintaining at 100% so you can come off it and there'll be no more saline drips till 4.00. But, you'll need another cannula because you're still on double antibiotics." Another cannula didn't sound much like good news, but he asked,

"So, the bad news...?"

"The bad news is..." At which point she fell upon him like a thug in a back street, grabbing a handful of his stomach and stabbing a hypodermic deep into it saying, "There, that wasn't so bad, was it? Oh, and I nearly forgot, you won't need another of those till tomorrow night." Her understanding of good news was different from his and seeing his expression, added, "You're lucky. I had one of those every day for three weeks after my daughter was born." *Mmm. Do that to me again and you'll die*, he thought. Then, after a pause, suggesting sympathetic solicitude,

"Is that all your news?"

"Think so."

"Hmm. *Well, no news is good news*," he supposed. Then, pondering, said, "I always misunderstood that phrase, thinking it meant all news is bad. Maybe I was right. How long have I been here?"

"Just over a week. Would you like the door closed?"

"Please. Can you turn the light off as well?"

"OK. Sleep if you can. Nothing more till 4.00 o'clock."

A week, he thought. Half an hour later...

"I've come to check your blood pressure. What's your date of birth again?"

Guards, shoot this woman!

The Truth of It.

Real voices returned to him like the rattle and chatter of coat hangers jangling and echoing in an empty wardrobe. He asked, "So, what is it I've got... had?" The answer came as a patois of ancient tongues, local dialects.

"It's complex. Difficult to explain in English..." declaimed the consultant at the foot of the bed. His gravitas, if not his stature, diminished by his unruly hairstyle. "You may have heard of Sepsis, but know this, my lad, you were close, this close," he demonstrated, bringing a large thumb and forefinger almost together.

"I couldn't have told the difference between a cannula and a catheter last week."

"If you had a cannula stuck in your cock," the big man said, "I can assure you, you would know the difference." You could tell how important he was from his size alone, which spoke volumes on his ability to dispense wisdom. His seniority, superscribed by his six young disciples, assiduously noting, on clipboards, his every utterance. No doubt they would resurface in dissertations in the years to come.

The truth is, he thought, hospital life had provided him with a lot to think about, like writing a short story. In this, his small piece of theatre, his ten days of suspended disbelief of voices on and off, with characters entering and departing stage right, he just kept swallowing the medicine along with his pride and everything else that went with his body being a bit of temporarily shared real estate. By the time he was given his marching orders to be transported away in a wheelchair, the pain was just about tolerable. But it was his pain, his alone and now, in his own reality he could take them both home with him.

SCABBED KNUCKLES

By Chris Kuriata

Ever since we moved in together, Vicki's knuckles are scabbed. Her skin looks like ice on a broken puddle. White lines run along her rough skin. The red lumps crack and leak. When I touch them, she lifts her chin, refusing to admit they ache.

"Who have you been fighting?" I ask, fully aware of the antagonistic people populating her job, her family, and the random sidewalk encounters during her long walks home through this dark neighbourhood. She doesn't want to fight, but others seek her out and force her.

Vicki takes my face in her hands, pretending they are still as soft and unblemished as when we first met. "No one," she says, and my heart breaks that she can lie to me so sincerely.

While Vicki is in the bathroom cleaning and spreading ointment over her battled knuckles, I fear we will not be together in another year's time. The skin around my knuckles is soft, and smells of our lavender soap. I do not want mine to match hers. When we hold hands, I do not want to feel as though I'm holding hands with myself.

*

I've put a cone on Kitten. His skin dries in the winter. He scratches and tears out clumps of fur until his bald back shines, all pink and glistening with pus, throbbing with infection. The pain is so bad I lay him in cardboard on the kitchen floor. He lies there for weeks, looking like he's dying. Vicki buys me a humidifier, and this winter when the scabs sprout on Kitten's back, he barely scratches, and they do not break open. The worst he gets is a quarter-sized patch beneath his chin the cone prevents him from raking his nails across and breaking open. He hates the cone. He meows incessantly, confused as to I am torturing him. The cone brings discomfort for Kitten and heartache for us.

I think of putting cones over Vicki's hands to keep her knuckles from getting worse. I'd have to tie the cones on when she's asleep. With both her hands encircled in deep plastic, her fingers couldn't reach the lace cords I'd do up in triple knots. My plan seems fool-proof, and I am already at the vets with a plastic cone in each hand, before I remember the dexterity of Vicki's toes, and the precision with which she can use her feet to pick up a pair of underwear and toss them across the bedroom into the laundry hamper. She does this so effortlessly, I imagine her dressed in a strongman's unitard performing this act in a circus ring before a crowd who bursts into applause before quieting down, breathlessly awaiting her next trick. A clown car bumbles into the ring, and when the door flies open a hundred angry faces bounce out, and Vicki socks each one in their vicious jaw, sending them soaring into the air and landing in the trapeze artist's net. Her scabbed knuckles drip blood into the sawdust floor.

*

At the lunch counter I have an accident with the grater. The carrot stump I'm gripping with my fingernails is too stubby, so when I'm laughing at the bawdiness of long-dead Lucille Bogan's song I'm distracted and rake my knuckles across the metal. My opened skin stings. It stings worse when I spray on the disinfectant that might as well be lemon juice. It stings again at the end of the night when I peel off the gloves I donned to keep things sanitary for the customers, lifting off the dried pus and scabs healing me over. Under my skin looks pink and glistening like Kitten's naked back last winter or like beneath his chin would were it not for the plastic cone. The plastic cone Vicki would so easily escape from.

That night in bed, Vicki runs her fingers over my cracked knuckles. "Who have you been fighting?" she asks. She sounds amused, like she's making a joke. A dirty joke. One where the laugh comes from anticipating my prudish reaction.

I steal her laughter, making her regret joking at my expense. "I punched a customer," I say. "He'd been in a lot. Had it coming." I roll over onto my side. "A Nazi."

She did not see my response coming. I expect her to roll over onto her own side, us back-to-back, so we can disappear in the dark and forget this conversation by morning.

Instead, she snakes her hand under the covers, rubbing her beaten knuckles against mine. The friction opens both our scabs. Our blood and pus mingle. Come morning, our grown over scabs will seal us together. Which one of us will reignite the sting by pulling away first to break them apart?

"I wish I'd been there," she says, sounding proud. She sounds like she wants to say more, perhaps confess the cause of her own beaten knuckles, but the moment collapses like the strands of a spider's web some tenacious insect manages to break free of. She stays silent, and soon she breathes the steady, unburdened rhythm of deep sleep.

A hollow clatter comes from the kitchen. Sounds like a dropped mixing bowl. Kitten meows, and I know he has finally managed to slip out of his cone. I guess his feet are as dexterous as Vicki's after all. I'm jealous. I wish my own feet were equal to my cat's and my girlfriend's. Kitten scratches, but I don't get out of bed to stop him. I no longer care if he opens the scab under his chin.

In her slumber, Vicki nestles close to me. I can hear the squish of her shifting eyes beneath her lids as she enters REM. She dreams of me punching Nazis, taking out three at a time with one Indiana Jones swing. She is proud my knuckles are scabbed like hers. I wish her knuckles could be more like mine. I fear we will not be together in a year's time.

DAMSELFLY
By Epiphany Ferrell

You used to love my iridescent wings. A double set, but only one set mobile. The other set droops down my back, tucked into my jeans. You used to tickle the still ones to make them quiver. I would fan your face with the good ones during sex.

"I can't even…" you said the other night, manoeuvring out from under me. "It's just so awkward!" And you rolled onto your side and fell asleep.

In the morning, I stood on the porch, resting my damp wings after my shower, letting the sun dry them. "I made coffee," I called through the screen door.

"I don't like coffee," you said.

You were the one who bought the coffee maker, the coffee grinder, instructed me on what coffee to buy at the co-op.

You came up behind me where I stood on the porch. "That one set doesn't even move," you said.

"I know."

"No, I mean, not at all. They used to quiver."

"When you'd tickle them."

"Might think about having them removed."

I fanned my good wings, the ones that do move.

"Can't even fly," he said. "I don't mean to be mean. But."

I moved the good ones softly, letting the sun rays undulate across them in purple and blue and turquoise. I put my shirt on, tucked my wings into my jeans.

You went into the garage to tinker with the motorcycle.

My still wings ache.

WINDMILL
By Justin Clement

You've been in Lagos for exactly twelve minutes and already you feel like retracing your elegant steps, your poised strides, back to the plane that brought you here. Before leaving Aberdeen, you'd felt that despite the fact that you haven't been in Nigeria since you were four years old, somehow your inner Nigerian would resonate with the land and adapt to it; the land of your birth, the land of your parents' and grandparents' birth.

Now, twelve minutes in, you are lightheaded with the oppressing, sweltering heat of the air, and you honestly wonder if the people here in Lagos are getting enough oxygen to breathe. Maybe it's why your aunt says everyone is mad here ("I'm not talking about the angry kind of mad, I mean mad mad! Even that person you're seeing in a suit is not well, but mad"). The breeze sending stray strands of your hair across your face is humid and warm, in a not-so-pleasant way. One side of your blue paisley-print handkerchief is already so damp that it annoys you to even hold it.

Things begin to look up when you're seated in a taxi, air-conditioned and speeding through Ikeja, en route to your aunt's house on the mainland. The air-conditioning cools the sweat on your forehead, and, you imagine, the sweat on your brain as well. The gaunt, yellow-eyed driver is chatty, overbearingly so, and you smile at his exuberant attempts to educate you on the workings of Lagos: *Madam, don't move around anyhow from eight at night. There are bad boys everywhere. Tinubu's boys are kidnapping people anyhow. Madam, this is your first time here, ba?* He talks and asks these questions with this comic nasal accent, and you smile and wonder if his jaw doesn't hurt as he speaks. You are unaware, that with your Scot-touched accent, and the aura of your Burberry perfume hovering around you as you rock that stylish black spaghetti top you like so much, he'd treated you like a textbook foreigner and charged you four times the normal fare. And so, like every outrageously priced establishment, he feels he must live up to the amount he charged you and deliver a wholesome, stellar service by talking, smiling all the time, and piling you with tons of seemingly needful information, in this case, on Life in Lagos 101, as if, somehow, these would justify his charge. But, as mentioned, you don't know all this.

You look out the window, at the passing cars—the flashy, the average, the jalopy. You feast your eyes on the passing buildings—the insalubrious, the mundane and the breathtaking. You look at the cringe-worthy and eye-catching surroundings and you wonder just how underdevelopment and development overlap and intertwine so easily, so seamlessly here.

This is the place of your birth, your first home. And now, twenty-five years after you left, you've returned to it.

*

You've been in Lagos for three days and you are still trying to understand the place, before throwing yourself into its maws. Your aunt's posh duplex is a slice of comfort and wellbeing, an oasis of quiet and peace. Ironic really, as your Aunt Chinenye is anything but quiet and peaceful. Portly, hyperactive, and readily available for a fistfight, even her sense of fashion speaks in noise—bright blue sandals, a neon-orange kaftan, and green headwear balanced atop her head, she reclines on the three-seat oxblood sofa as she goes through your phone's music library.

"*Biko*, Adaeze, what kind of songs are these and who are these musicians? Wildes? London Grammar? Of Monsters and Men? Are you sure you're listening to mankind?" She laughs and laughs and rolls her eyes, before stretching your phone out to you. "*Ha*, Scotland has turned your head around."

"Those are good musicians, Aunty," you utter as you take your phone, your dignity in a bit of a fix. "Plus, they're not even Scottish bands."

"Okay *o*, if you say so," she says, shrugging. "You should listen to some Nigerian artistes. Like Wizkid, Burna Boy, Davido and the others. I can write you a list of them if you want."

"Okay, Aunty. You can write me a list of the ones you like later," you say, sighing. Everything feels disorienting here, so different from what you know — even the music. One disorienting thing you've come to like and look forward to however, is the food. It plays with your taste buds, engages them in an orchestra of delicious spiciness. You remember how your aunt laughed when you lifted the teaspoon to your lips to taste the egusi soup she made the day you arrived. She'd laughed to tears and asked who took egusi soup with a spoon while the garri sat in the plate beside it, steaming. The explosion of taste and flavour on your tongue made you forgive her for making fun of you.

"You know you still haven't really said why you came back," Aunt Chinenye says. "Because even me, I don't know why you would leave Europe and return to Nigeria. And you've been giving me very, very vague reasons. Reasons that I cannot even remember."

"Aunty," you say, taking a seat on the adjacent sofa. "I told you I came here to start afresh."

"Afresh *kwa*? Doesn't Scotland have better prospects than here?"

"It does but... not really in the way I would want."

"And what way is that?" Aunt Chinenye asks, raising an eyebrow.

"It's complicated, Aunty. Closure, I guess."

"*Chai*. God help me *o*," Aunt Chinenye mutters and smiles. "You sound just like a white person."

"I've been abroad for a really long while. A really long while, Aunty," you say, with exaggerated gesticulations. You both burst into laughter. In the midst of your mirth however, her words begin to turn over in your head. *You sound just like a white person.* The words burrow into your mind, your heart, and you know somehow, inexplicably, that you will remember those words for the rest of your life. It dampens your mood, those words, and you imagine just how much of a foreigner you really sound like, how out of touch you are with your own country. These words will form the basis for your metamorphosis, for that long journey of self on the road to becoming what you will feel is Nigerian.

*

You've been in Lagos for two weeks and right now, you find yourself in a market. The place assaults you. Not a subtle affront on your physical senses, no, but a full-scale, stupefying attack. The discordant voice of the market stuns you, the organized chaos shakes you and you think about how your chances of fainting have just skyrocketed.

Though you don't intend or want to, you begin to compare what you see with what you have seen. You superimpose images of the neat walkways of interlocked stone at the few markets in Aberdeen you've been to onto the muddied footpaths you see now, surrounded by insalubrious, makeshift stalls on all sides. Even the amalgam of colour here is different, more in-your-facey, and you put a hand on your aunt's shoulder as your eyes swim lightly.

"Adaeze, what is wrong?" your aunt asks as she stops and turns, lifting an eyebrow as she tilts her head. "Are you well?"

You take a deep breath and try to smile. "I'm fine, Aunty. I'm just… taking it all in."

"Taking it all in *kwa*? What is there to take in at a market? Scotland has no markets or what?" she says and resumes walking. You follow her and silently wonder why she didn't simply buy the foodstuffs today at any of the numerous grocery stores around the estate.

"Hold your bag in front of you and hold it well," your aunt quickly tells you.

"Oh. Yes." You readjust your bag and refer to other tidbits your aunt has dropped on you these two weeks you've been with her. *If you ever want to buy something at the market, whatever the seller says, insist on getting it half the price or something close; Don't mind all those fine Fulani children that will even hug you tightly as they're begging for alms. Bone your face and ignore them. Many of them are not really poor; Always hold your phone in your hand. If you keep it in your pocket in some places, then sorry is your name.*

You watch your aunt haggle, and you wonder when the word 'haggle' became synonymous with 'yelling match.' As far as you could tell, Aunt Chinenye was gesturing to some succulent, leafy vegetables set before her, shouting at, and asking why the seller didn't just rob her at gunpoint instead of fixing such flagrant prices. The seller was also viciously arguing, almost swearing even, how her prices were fair and cheap. Just when you feel that the verbal sparring match would devolve into blows, the seller begins placing some of the vegetables in a black polyethylene bag, and hands it over to Aunt Chinenye. After she pays and thank yous are exchanged, she turns and winks at you as she makes her way to another stall, with you following closely. "If you do soft-soft, these people will just cheat you anyhow. They can even sell you, *sef*."

"What?" you blurt, eyes wide.

"Figure of speech *o*," your aunt says, laughing lightly. "It's just an expression."

"Oh. I see." You feel ashamed that for a minute, you assumed that her words were literal. It makes you feel traitorous, and to some tiny degree, racist.

Could someone be racist to their own race? Your brows furrow slightly.

*

You've been in Lagos for four months and now you feel this permeating ache within you, a cloying kind of hurt. Everywhere and everything radiates hostility or, at best, indifference. You begin to see yourself as someone unworthy of being Nigerian, as someone so far detached from their roots. It's like a dissociation really, a dawning knowledge of being unfettered, and gradually, you begin to feel the phantom connection you had with the land fraying.

With the merlot on the table before you a quarter gone, and the soothing purr of the air conditioner of your aunt's ornate living room, you decide to be in sync with the country of your birth. This place would not subdue you or force you docile. You make up your mind to rise above everything. No matter how long it had been since you've been away, you're a Nigerian by birth, by blood. You thank God for good wine.

In the following weeks and months, you mentally begin to award points to yourself for anything you do that you feel makes you more Nigerian. When you out-yell the sellers at the market and get them to agree with your stated price, your inner self grins in wicked delight and you resist the urge to raise a fist in the air. When you stand in front of Aunt Chinenye's full-length mirror, perfecting your stoic face, a paragon of the resting bitch syndrome, you suppress the giggles that lie just below your throat as you stare daggers into the mirror. Behind the windows of her Honda, you test run your new Lagos face. With one hand on the steering wheel, you never once glance at the caramel-skinned biracial children that latch themselves to the car windows, mouths forming inaudible pleas as they peer into the vehicle as if searching for something. Hope, maybe? When the traffic light goes green and you leave the child beggars behind, the face falters and you wonder where those giggles that lay in your mouth had gone.

You begin to practice the local pidgin; the harsh sounding yet somewhat lyrical distortion of the English language. Speaking it feels like a burden, a weight. But it is a weight you're determined to carry, to bench-press if need be.

"Say it like this: where *you* dey?" Aunt Chinenye says, while she uses a finger to lightly tap the lit cigarette between her fingers, watching the ash fall into the tray on the sofa's arm.

"Where. You. Day?"

Aunt Chinenye gives a hearty, guttural laugh, a laugh you feel must shake up her internal organs. "You still talk like a Scot," she says, as she wipes tears from an eye with a manicured finger. "I have not heard this kind of pidgin before. What posh pidgin."

You sigh. "But honestly. 'Where are you' is also three words. Why not just say that one instead?"

"I don't know *o*, Adaeze. I'm not the one that fabricated the pidgin. Na so I see am."

You make up your mind to lose the Scottish tinge to your voice, though you will miss its high lightness, like cotton candy in the mouth.

King's Daughter. That's what your name means. Not surprisingly, as you muse on its meaning now, you feel nothing like a daughter of a king. You are the daughter of no one, orphaned a few years ago when your parents died in the helicopter crash. You still do not tell your aunt that you returned to Nigeria to find the connection—that tether that grounded you to something special, something of home—that was ripped from you with your parents' passing.

You do not tell Aunt Chinenye that you desperately crave your country's acceptance—a full body and soul assimilation into its fibre— because you cannot bear to be adrift endlessly anymore. Your father told you once that no person can be a stranger in their own land. It was one of those proverbs he uttered when his belly was full of your mother's dish of spiced chicken gizzards, and you felt in the mood to humour his faux sage persona, on those evenings spent in front of the fireplace.

Now you think of how wrong he was, how jarringly inaccurate his words were. Stranger describes you perfectly here, aptly so. You wonder what other parts of yourself you have to let go of to become one with the land of your origin. You also think of what the land will give you, what you have to take in, and also just how much you can accept. You think of the years ahead, and you wonder just how you will survive the jaws of the place that seems bent on swallowing you whole.

You are in the land of your birth, yet you do not feel home. You feel yourself breaking; breaking to become, breaking to belong. You call it your metamorphosis, your gradual transformation and adaptation. You will become Nigerian. You will reach for it and hold on to it with all your strength.

Even if she has to rewrite herself completely, till what is left is a ropy mass of scribbled lines.

CHESTER BEATTY'S LONELY HEARTS CLUB BAND

By Sahar Ahmed

I don't hear the azaan in Dublin. I can't hear the azaan in Dublin. Except on the top floor of the Chester Beatty. The sound is soft at first, periodic, interlaced with distinctly different sounds of bells and chanting. But the further in you walk through the doors, the louder and clearer it becomes. It abruptly stops, before it's supposed to. Muscle memory tells me that there should be at least another minute of it – and it *is* muscle memory because I know that sound with my whole body. I don't think I've ever just heard the azaan, I've always physically reacted to it. There is a series of automatic motions that always happens when I hear the azaan – the music or tv is turned down, there is a momentary pause in conversation, a dupatta is taken over the head to cover it (or if I am being perfectly honest, I am prodded to do this last one, it has never happened voluntarily). I don't even think I am very aware of it anymore except in the way that the mind is always aware of the things that bring it comfort. But none of those things happen inside the Chester Beatty. Just as abruptly as it stops, the sound is heard again, and this cyclical start and stop continues all day. It's strange and beautiful and I love it.

I moved from Pakistan to Dublin, Ireland in 2016, and one of the first places I visited as I got to know the city was the Chester Beatty Library. One of the most famous museums in the country, it houses a wonderful, diverse collection, with manuscripts, rare books, and art from across the world's religious cultures and traditions. But unlike, for example, the Victoria and Albert Museum in London, the Chester Beatty really leans into the 'engagement' part of its mission statement –"To care for, research, share and promote the Chester Beatty collections fostering understanding, engagement and curiosity", something you can hear the tour guides around the museum talking about too; phrases like 'multicultural', 'learning from one another', 'shared rich histories' are used often. A private-collection-turned-public-museum, it's small but not too small. And it's on every 'Must-see when visiting Dublin' list.

But I don't remember my first trip to it. I'm sure it was a good experience – I must have really liked the place because I recommended it to every person who visited me from anywhere in the world over the next few years. I even think I went back a number of times, whether it was to meet a friend for coffee in the café, or to kill time while waiting for someone nearby. But what I do remember vividly is not going beyond the first floor.

The first floor gallery, Arts of the Book, houses (as the name suggests) a stunning collection of rare books, historical printing artefacts, and the like. There is an entire section that showcases some of the most decadent and ornate copies of the *Qur'an*, exquisite leather binding and covers for *Qur'an* printed and made in Egypt in the 15th century, stunning compilations of *Hadith*, produced in Shiraz, Iran in 1435. The list is long, and I can keep calling it stunning and beautiful and wonderous, and it would all be true. I remember really liking this floor. It had a lot of non-Islamic material too, with book history and culture from East Asia, Europe, and Biblical printing history. But all of it felt very… close to home. I was a Muslim girl, from Pakistan, I was there in Dublin to do a PhD in law and religion, and having lived in London before, I was *done* with stuff that felt too familiar. My head and heart both knew I had so much religion and religion-adjacent research ahead of me in the coming years – did I really need to be spending so much free time looking at related histories? I did not know this at the time, but I was already growing tired of playing the part of a 'good' scholar, Arabizing my Islam for the sake of academia. My Islam was not liturgical and italicised, and I had started to miss it. Plus, wasn't I done with seeing things white dudes took from my land and housed in white countries? I was. And so, I wandered the first floor, admired the collection, and left.

It's been six years now since I moved to Ireland. I've finished that PhD through much personal sacrifice, enduring endless racism from within the academy, my institution, my discipline… my temporary 'home'. I also got married. I married the most incredible Irish man, who has filled my life with a love and friendship unlike any I have ever experienced before. He makes me happy. And yet, the months that followed our grand wedding(s!) across countries and continents, have been filled with a strange sadness. I chalked it up to post-PhD depression, or that void that one feels the day after a big party when the house is quiet and empty. But during one of our sessions, my therapist and I got talking about the future, my desire to have children, how I want to raise my family, and my anxieties around the 'practical' decisions I was debating making – namely, whether to change my name or not. I've heard so many stories from black and brown friends with white children, who keep having trouble when travelling without their white partners at immigration, being stopped and questioned mindlessly because the surnames on their passports don't match – mothers accused of 'stealing' their children. And these stories have terrified me.

I find myself going from never having even conceived of the notion that I might have to take any future husband's name, to feeling like I have to. I didn't realise it was bothering me so much. I'm so happy being married to my best friend, we have the best time in our home together, we're building a life we're both proud of, and I knew it would be like this from the second we got engaged. The idea that I could feel anything other than absolute joy was so bizarre that I didn't let myself process what this means. Because of how identity is recorded in my home country, (a fraught topic for another day), I'm having to change my status on my Pakistani ID card. It records me as my father's daughter – I am 'daughter of'. Now it needs to say 'wife of' – my father's name will be removed. We've decided to live in Ireland (at least for the foreseeable future), which means I have had to reconcile with not being with my ageing parents in Lahore when they die. (I lie. I haven't reconciled with it at all.) I have to also come to terms with how Ireland is no longer a 'temporary' home, but a permanent one, and that means accepting that I have to live with both its beauty and its ugliness – that racism and Islamophobia I've endured since arriving will now be a constant feature of my life.

I am overwhelmed.

I went back to the Chester Beatty one day in June. I was once again killing time before meeting some friends for lunch. It was really hot (for

Ireland) and so I was wearing a shalwar kameez made of lawn, the cool fabric we wear all summer long in Pakistan. And I strolled in feeling very lost, and looking a bit too much like a 'foreigner'... a tourist, maybe? I did my walk around the first floor gallery, as usual, and then decided to do something different. I went upstairs. The second floor gallery, 'Sacred Traditions', "exhibits the sacred texts, illuminated manuscripts and miniature paintings from the great religions and systems of belief represented in the collections", says their website. And there was the faint azaan, soft and periodic, interlaced with bells and chanting. I made a beeline for the back of the 'Islam' section, where the sound was coming from, and wept. I'm known to cry very easily and frequently but even I hadn't sobbed in a museum before. I cried till my body grew tired of doing so. I didn't want to forget the feeling, so I took out my phone to make a note of it and let myself type "I heard the azaan today". Not the *adhan* I write about in my scholarship: I let myself feel the azaan in Urdu. I let myself feel sad for knowing that I am choosing a future in a place where I will only hear it at the Chester Beatty.

THE SILENT WOMAN

By Olivia Payne

An eye meets my eye, coming from a face which is firm, flesh sitting smoothly, fitting tightly onto bone. The hair is also controlled, curled like a waiting predator on this rock face. It is a trick, I know, because it is dead. This hair is better than a crocodile, better than a possum.

"Does she not speak?" the face, which belongs to the eye, asks. The other only laughs. He would not make me speak.

"It looks just like her!" another face says reproachfully. I have never seen something, a discrete and whole thing, that looks like me. Many different things, yes. I can see parts of myself in the rug on the floor, or a fur coat, the chair that coat is now lying on, the paintbrushes in the studio. The paintings supposedly of me, hanging on the walls, are missing something. Although, they are art so perhaps they are adding something – either way they are not equal to my being.

Others all duly come and observe me as they arrive. The silent woman, as I'm called. They chatter around and about me, some turning immediately to the paintings of me, the silent image. They must see it as well, the discrepancy between me and the image, but then many of them also know this third thing, this other being, this 'her' who is 'me', as well. And when they look at me, they're thinking of her. And when he looks at me, he is thinking of her. Many times, he has asked me-her-us "Alma, where did I go wrong?", this even whilst his arms were around my form. Many times he has asked me to talk for this someone else, and never do I, nor can I, answer. He doesn't wait for an answer, either.

Now he straightens me up, and adjusts my dress, my hair, before leaving me amongst his living guests. I am human-sized, as they might put it, but I cannot stand, so I sit beneath their gazes. Instead, I am eye-level with silks, lace, feathers. These heavy bodies press around me, intercut with the steps of men lightly bearing trays, softly breaking groups apart who reform again *in the wake. They wait until he leaves, at least, to talk about me. And, of course, that is why he has left.*

*

"No, but...does he make love to her?"

"It is art, Max, it is art!"

"Well, let us not forget that suitor of the stone, that man – why has history forgotten his name? – that man who became the lover of that most divine work of Praxiteles, that radical inventor who beat Pygmalion at his own game –"

"It is ugly art," I say, and the words roll awkwardly from my mouth.

"Well, there's a paradox!"

"Max is a realist, I'm afraid," Hilda laughs as she places a hand on my arm. She was forever using that word in an inappropriately straightforward way to mean someone who uses facts. Or, in other words, not what she would call an artist. An artist, therefore, is a kind of irrealist. Unrealist. An unrealiser of things, who unravels both himself and the world as he goes through it.

"Of course, he can't afford not to be!"

"Max always needs some clear boundaries, don't you Max?"

It suddenly occurred to me that she used my name incorrectly as well, wielding it as a heavy club of intimacy.

"I'm only following the example of God, who gave me skin."

"Oh, that's beneath you Max, really, bringing in God."

As usual, she misunderstood my intention. I really wanted to ask about the skin of the doll. Otto had been very particular about it in his many, many, letters to its maker, and I wanted to know what had caused the sudden change of vision. Those angry, awkward, feathers –

"No, no. He has a point. When we cut ourselves it is painful, is that pain perhaps a reflection of man's difficulty of exposing himself to the experience of the other? Is it a necessary pain we must push past?"

"There's no need to get philosophical about physical reality. Bodily pain keeps us from repeating harmful mistakes, it's purely evolutionary."

"Can she feel pain, do you reckon?" I jerk my head at the doll. Wilhelm picks up a knife from a sideboard and pushes towards the figure, laughing as he is restrained by Hilda. He lets her push against him, push the sharp nails of her small hands into his skin, she is panting with effort as he anticipates her clumsy assaults.

"Don't Will! Don't hurt it." I feel a surge of some emotion for Hilda as our aims align. Perhaps she was having an influence on me, if I – the businessman realist – could imagine a doll having feelings, like a little girl would.

"You must know it is Otto's intention to destroy it this evening."

"It is? But –" They didn't hear me, caught in their own game.

"And you must know, *Wilhelm*, that sacrificial victims are to be treated with honour at all times in the hours before their death."

"Ah, she is right. She is right – I had forgotten."

"You've become estranged from the life of the common man, that's why, Will."

"That's uncalled for, Max."

"A hit! A very palpable hit!" I continue, "success has cut him off from the cultic –"

"Ignore him Will, he's a child using words found in his father's papers."

"Your papers more like."

"Yes, Hil, how's your latest coming along?"

Of course, I wasn't expected to follow this conversation about craft. Wilhelm and Hilda shrugged off their flirtation to talk about the heavens, the muse, the calling, the purpose, the plastic. I could stare freely at the doll. Otto the great artist had commissioned a lesser woman artist to make a doll made of dead things to be another living woman artist. It did not resemble any woman. I felt certain of this even though I had never met the original. Alma Mahler – I knew her through her husband's music. I had seen her in my ears, and she was beautiful there. Too beautiful, I thought, for Otto. But an artist needn't ascertain the reality of the world around him as a realist does. So, he can make an ugly doll of a beautiful woman. And you cannot ask if or how he makes love to a doll. You cannot even ask do you want me to come to this party with you Hilda, yes or no? Do you need some money Hilda? What do these other men want with you Hilda? These are irrelevant questions for an artist, and Hilda would only be indulging my childish naïveté if she answered.

When the party moves outside, we find the garden filled with flowers and statues. Ever the barbarian, Otto surrounded himself with lovelier things than he himself could produce. He had hired a chamber orchestra for the evening, in the full formal wear that he and many of his guests scorned, and the beauty of their music was chilled by the nature of the farce they had found themselves in. An elegant dining chair had been dragged onto the lawn and sat afront the fountain. It was for the doll. When she came out, the guest of honour, it took her handler several tries to make her sit upright upon her burnish'd throne, the weight of her heavy limbs slumping downwards. From a distance, as we ate, she seemed like a Spanish widow in her black, cloaked in her sad, silent stillness.

*

I am offered bits of meat from their forks, teasingly. They do not know how far the mirror goes, if I have a throat, a gullet, a stomach, behind my teeth and tongue. Wine is spilled onto my dress. It had been a struggle to be put into the dress, my form is so unaccommodating, it seems, to others. I felt it ruined, the wine soaking through it into my skin, my skin turning red, my insides turning red, and outside me in sympathy their faces around me also slowly turning red with wine.

The air of the garden ruffles my skin. He has left me unprotected. The mocking looks I have seen from afar, in the restaurants, in the opera house, as they walked by me in the street, are now upon me. They play with me: a game to test our similarity. A woman presses her face to what she considers my face, covering her hair with mine. Another presses our palms together. Palm to palm is holy palmer's kiss, a man says. This opens the way for another man to kiss my mouth. Someone opens my mouth and counts my teeth. They take me out of the chair, and I am danced, passed around from hand to hand, in time to the music, fast and unfamiliar music.

*

The doll is thrust into my hands by a laughing Wilhelm. Hilda has already danced with her, amusing everyone by acting the man, taking the lead, and pretending to kiss her, and she shrieks as I cannot repress a jolt upon

THE SILENT WOMAN

receiving her. The doll is as tall as I am, heavy and awkward to hold, and the feathered skin slips through my hands. She had been fully dressed for the occasion – Otto even informed us that he had ordered undergarments specially from Paris. If it wasn't for the feathers underneath you might be able to close your eyes and feel just that dress, the silk that is the shorthand for a live woman in your hands. It takes a great effort to twirl her round while the others clap the frantic rhythm of the polka, and her unsupported head flops forward and backward – it is a danse macabre, I think, although there is still flesh on the corpse.

"The champagne – I'm too dizzy –" I excuse myself, but find that she is still with me, I have been unable to fulfil my duty to offload her onto the next pair of hands. Typical Max, ruining the joke. It would be much easier if Otto hadn't given her those eyes, if he had perhaps had a pair embroidered flat onto her face.

"Come on Max, give her back to us!"

But I drag her farther away. I can hardly look at her. Is this really Alma? Is this the woman I had heard? She was whispered about, shouted about. Beautifully, terribly alive. What had Otto captured here?

"It's worn out – it's served its purpose, I see that now," Otto had approached me silently, that sharp face, looking down into the doll's large eyes. They weren't blank like the small, glass marbles I remember my sister cooing over, in the waxy heads of her small dolls. These were knowing. How had the artist instilled them with knowing, even if seen apart from the rest of the face's expression, if you held up your hand to block everything but the eyes from view?

"Will you close its eyes, at least, Otto, before you kill her?"

"I don't think I will need to."

But he was still looking into her eyes, *elle a des yeux, de vrais yeux, des yeux vivants, des yeux de flame, des yeux merveilleux* – Hilda had refused to come with me to see Coppélia, as she would refuse to see any ballet, any music not sanctioned or created by her own circle. A whole world filtered only through one lens. Even the sword at Otto's side must have been suggested to him, found for him, attached unnaturally to his flabby side. Nothing will come of nothing, but somehow Otto had found a way. He had cheated.

*

"Yes, it's served its purpose."

I seem to have completed a task of some kind, and I do not know how, when I cannot do a thing for myself. I cannot even close my eyes. I remember my maker, who perhaps knew my purpose, as she sewed together my skin, stuffed my body, plucked my eyes from a table and put them in. She gathered me together, with slow deliberation, nothing left to chance, in her workshop. There were other dolls, smaller dolls, there, that she had also made. Her purpose, it seems, was in making them. And the man's in having me. Or remaking me, flattening me onto canvas. And my original, her purpose was in being made into me?

I see the men struggle against each other weakly. Even though they have bones and muscle and energy, their forms are clumsy and unsure. An excited crowd gathers, they pull each other over. Here was unlooked-for, additional violence for them to observe. The music stops as the men who make it also rush and mingle into the crowd.

I have seen it hanging on the wall, much as it used to hang on another wall in some other world, before it was fetched into ours, still sharp and unmoving and beautiful. I did not know that he would be using the sword. But I know already, before he throws the other off, before he is sawing at my neck, that it won't come easily. I was made too well for that. He is forced to give up ceremony and use his hands, his own hands, to tear at the remains of my neck. And now my body is here, and my head is there, and my horse-hair and feathers, as usual, are between.

"Murderer!" the other shouts, even though – surely, he can see – that I am still all here.

He picks up my head and looks into my eyes. His are crying. But mine were not made to do so.

WINDOW

By Justin Rigamonti

Kurt walked into a wave of sadness whenever he left the minimart on 12th and Cook. Wasn't sure why. He'd stiffen his upper body, inhale as though he were going to fight it, then sigh and float on top. Ride the sadness like its goddamn captain.

No particular image set him off: the blinking lotto lights, the green and red advertisements. And no particular smell: old corndogs, stale cigarettes. He felt the swivel at the start of it, like a saloon door in a western, the subtle shift in the breeze before the mood descended.

Dark water filled his limbs, an oceanic glow. Maybe the sense of having sinned, in the minimart, by virtue of having been in a minimart, which he thought of as low-brow, pathetic. Maybe the peeling branches of the sycamore outside, or the crooked gate behind Ship Ahoy, or the blue-lit man in the window across Gladstone, eating something.

Microwave popcorn this time. "Butterlovers." Which he chose because she always wanted extra butter, Donna. She loved things like that. The worst kinds of butter, too, movie theatre butter, possibly toxic. He said the words in his head, possibly toxic, working his jaw as he thought of her. Squeezed it, jostled the bone. Felt the warm leather of his own skin. The transfer of sensation where his fingertips connected with his cheek, capillary-rich flesh awash in light.

He thought about her back, the blue-green lines of her tattoo, the pink heat of her skin, the open pores, oil under his hands, he thought of her turning in the bed beneath him, a glossy streak across her shoulder blade, the side of her face like a sun coming into view. He paused and listened. Then he sighed and reached again into the popcorn bag. Like clockwork, the neighbour kid walked past the window, twentysomething, with that glum look on his face, like he was about to sink into the concrete, like he'd just found out this was it, right here, this was everything.

AND ALSO WITH YOU

By Lea Mc Carthy

And Also *with* You.

 I always sat at the back of the church and I don't remember how that began. I'm certain there wasn't a choice given but I don't think it was an order. I doubt I did it as a proud refusal. It was just a seat, in the beginning.

 My classmates, of course, were gathered around the front, rows of pews ahead of me. I would watch the backs of their heads, some of them slumped and bored, others sitting up rapt with attention. The priest addressed the class from the pulpit, so him, I could see. Because of the distance, I couldn't hear clearly what was going on in those Tuesday morning Eucharist classes. I never really learned the ins and outs of the first Holy Communion.

 All of my religious education (as the only child out of thirty not receiving the sacrament, due to a difference of religious opinion) was found in the call-and-responses which rang out loud enough to reach my back pew.

 "The Lord be with you!"

 "And also with you!"

 While my classmates chorused in earnest and played hymns on the recorder and stumbled through readings from the Holy Bible, I kicked my light-up shoes against the pew. The lessons seemed to span for hours. Still now, I know the church off by heart, all the time spent mulishly staring into space. The leaflets in muted colours with lots of exclamation points, pinned up on the noticeboard by the door. The curious stone sink that Teacher dipped her fingers into: and some particularly pious kids copied her. The inside of the church itself: vast, cold, and cavernous. The walls were peppered with the stations of the cross, a picture story spread out in neat black frames. I had to avert my eyes from it, or I'd feel the painful sting of the nails in my palms.

 The windows were the best part. Holy Communion classes were in the morning, the exact right time to see the stained glass animated by sunlight, casting jewel coloured light onto the floor, pools of reds and greens. It was quite holy and rather terrifying. At the time, the word *blessing* had never been quite explained to me, though I heard it mentioned frequently. Naturally I came to the conclusion that perhaps it was the action word for when a window bleeds onto the floor.

The people in the windows weren't bothered that their colours ran. They looked nothing like us in our grey uniforms, or Teacher, they even overshadowed the priest in his karate-kit shroud (I heard if you lie during your first confession, he kicks you in the face, *ki-yah!*). The window-people were draped in layers of richness, an abundance of colour and folds. In one hand, they almost invariably carried some strange, mystical object and with the other hand, they held up their fingers in secret signals. On particularly good days, when the sun flooded the windows and the colours blessed themselves onto the floor, I thought perhaps it would bring the window people back to life and march a procession of velvet cloaked saints across the cold floor. The signals they made with their creaking, bent fingers were for me to join them, they'd allow me to parade with them, all the way up to the front at last.

About halfway through the year of the communion classes, I realised this would never happen. The eyes told me. The window-people had the most downturned, miserable eyes you've ever seen. If people knew they were due to come back to life, they'd be much happier.

"Body of Christ!"

"This is my body!"

I made eye contact with the priest as he held up a small white circle. Body of Christ was one of those phrases repeated constantly. What was the body of Christ? Where was the body of Christ? Christ belonged to that priest anyway, that was certain. The priest probably was the one to bury Christ himself, out in the graveyard that spread out in the shadow of the church. I imagined the priest digging, dirtying his karate-kit, wiping sweat off his perfect forehead. Then he would have wiped his hands clean, made the sign of the cross, and started spreading the word to all the local children. How else could he have come to be so revered? And now, the body of Christ lay there, curled up like a sleeping giant. I traced the shape in my mind; he fit perfectly. His knees would be tucked up against the gate, his shoulders were traced by the long winding path up to the church doors. Which would mean the head of Christ was in the church. No. The head of Christ *was* the church.

While I came to this ephiphany, my classmates lined up in front of the priest. Teacher fished around in her handbag and took out a share bag of white chocolate buttons. She gave them to the priest. (In the future, I would realise that the chocolate buttons were standing in for sacramental bread. There was simply not enough Body of Christ to go around.) As each child approached the priest, they mumbled something to him, and were given a chocolate button in return. I licked my lips at the thought of one and tried to refocus on my discovery.

Once I realised we were all within the head of Christ, I was seeing things more clearly. The long brown crucifix on the back wall was his nose. Those two ornate pillars were long weeping eyes, pierced in the middle with two smaller black crosses, like pupils. The alter was his top lip, the long wine-coloured carpet that ran from pulpit to back door was his tongue; it explained the colour. The rows of hard, heavy pews were his teeth. Which meant that I, right at the back, was sitting in God's wisdom tooth.

And then it came to me suddenly. Out of boredom, I've been kicking the pews with my scuffed runners.

I've been kicking God in the teeth.

The dread ran down my body, *he must have it in for me now*. My class was reciting the Lord's prayer – I'd never learned it, but I'd heard it chanted so many times that I was sure I knew it by heart. Perhaps it would appease God to hear me. I whispered under my breath:

"Our Father,

Who are in heaven, hello be die name,

Die kingdom come, die will be done,

On earth as it is in heaven.

Give us this day, or they'll leave bread;

and forgive us our dressed passes,

as we forgive those who dress pass against us;

and lead us not into temp-tation,

but deliver us from evil.

Eamon."

What a boy called Eamon had to do with God, Jesus Christ and the Holy Spirit, I wasn't quite sure, but it was the done thing to say.

When the class finished the prayer, the priest gave out to them because they ran through it too quickly, like auctioneers. He made them promise they'd do the Mary prayer better. I knew they wouldn't. There's something about a prayer that you just want to say it all at once, as quickly as possible.

I was sweating bullets now, my heart hammering. Teacher started walking down the carpeted aisle towards me, as if she knew. I wanted to scream at her to stop, she was chopping up God's tongue with her high heels, stamping down his mouth to get to me. He was sure to think it was my fault. The church smelt like dusty cough drops and anger.

Teacher patted me on the shoulder and gave me the leftover chocolate buttons from the share bag. I put one in my mouth and sucked it miserably, listening to the next chanting of prayer. The Mary prayer. I despaired all the more on hearing it. That last line:

"Holy Mary, mother of God

Pray for us sinners,

Now and at the- Agrrhhh! - of our death."

That's when I learned that I'd be dying with an *agrrhhh*. There would be no quiet deaths; only savage, screaming ones. Violent death was promised by the Mary prayer. If you've been good, and listened to the priest, and not said your prayers like an auctioneer, and read your readings from the holy bible, she'll pray for you and try stop the *agrrhhh* of your death, block it with her superpowers. There'd be no prayers for me, no hope, after all I'd been kicking Jesus in the teeth, I never learned a single prayer from a book, and I wasn't even good enough to be let sit near the front.

I sat in God's wisdom-tooth, waiting for the *agrrhhh* of my death, and I watched the windows bless themselves again, and bleed all over the hardwood floor.

EXTRAORDINARY

By Don Noel

James decided on his eighteenth birthday that he would no longer respond to "Jim". He had spent the day driving aimlessly around town in his second-hand grey Toyota imagining things that might separate him from ordinariness, and the forename thing came to him: a useful first step.

"This is James Allen," friends should henceforth say in introducing him at parties. "James, not Jim, please." People who that night also met Pete or Joe or Hal might not remember them, but they would remember James Allen, and someday think of him when they needed important things done, unusual things. Extraordinary things.

To reinforce the message, he bought a paint kit and changed the Toyota's fenders from grey to electric blue. Even from a block away, the car was unmistakable. People would identify that car with James Allen.

In the ensuing decade, though, his life continued to be depressingly humdrum: He took courses at the community college, got a job as a bank teller, met the co-ed who became his wife, bought a house with a white picket fence, and began a family, a boy and a girl. He nonetheless never abandoned his ambition to escape the unexceptional. When the time came for a newer used car, he had its fenders, too, painted electric blue.

And then one Saturday morning he was pleased to find on his doorstep a stranger who could only have come to see this unusual fellow who insisted on being called by his full and proper name. Having had a look, the man beat a hasty retreat with an improbable alibi that piqued James' curiosity. It was the sort of doorstep observation, he mused later, that the FBI might employ in vetting a candidate for an important post.

This is how it went: he had come to the door to see what FedEx had brought. The deliveryman routinely left James' packages on the front porch, rang the doorbell and went on to his next stop. By the time James got downstairs, the truck was always long gone.

This morning the doorbell rang twice, the second time just as he reached the foot of the stairs. Opening the door, James found himself face-to-face with the maybe-FBI man, in jeans and a sweat jacket whose official-looking lettering was obscured by a bright blue windbreaker. A FedEx package was at his feet.

James wished that before opening the door he had put on his dress Stetson, as if on his way to something important. The hat had a memorably wider brim than most Easterners wore. "Hello," he said. "What are you..." He stifled that opening, wanting to make clear he was someone who took unusual happenings in stride, and began again. "Can I help you?"

"Oh, thank you," said the man. He stepped back to glance beside the door at the house number, in the great looping brass numerals James had bought for their originality. "I'm looking for 324 Buckingham Street. I have the right number, but maybe this isn't right."

"No," James said, "you're on Edgewood Street. Buckingham is almost downtown."

"I'm sorry. Can you point us in the right direction?"

James realized there was a car in the driveway, a second man behind the wheel. "It's almost two miles. I'd go to the end of the block here and take a right onto East Main. After about a mile, when you cross Evergreen – perhaps the fifth or sixth traffic light – you ought to stop and ask someone. You'll be near."

"Got it. Thanks." The man walked to the driveway, spoke through an open window to the man driving – relaying James' instructions, no doubt – then walked around to the passenger-side door. They backed out of the driveway and headed off in the direction James had suggested.

He mentioned the incident to Susan when she got home from grocery shopping with the kids. "Something quite unusual happened while you were away," he said. He described the encounter. "Someone had sent that man to look me over. To see if I was rattled to find a stranger on the doorstep. I can't wait to see what happens next."

"Oh, James!" she sighed. It was a tone she used from time to time, which he understood as acknowledging one or another of his extraordinary qualities.

For the next few days, he declined to stifle his cell phone in places and on occasions where one normally did so, but neither the maybe-FBI man nor anyone else called.

"Oh, look!" said Susan at the breakfast table one morning. "It's a good thing you came to the door the other day. We might have lost the package." She thrust a newspaper page at him.

Thieves had begun following delivery trucks, the article said, pulling in at random to see if anyone came to the door where packages had been left. If not, they came up and rang the doorbell. "If still no one comes, they grab the package and skedaddle," a police spokesman was quoted. There seemed to be more than one pair running this scam. Two or three. "We need the public's help to catch these guys."

Susan did not mention his earlier theory about the man who had come to their door, so James did not have to revisit that perhaps-mistaken idea. Rather, he saw an opportunity to make a difference because he was expecting another package soon. He set out a pad and pencil by the front door and spent a few minutes practicing taking pictures with his phone. He also went online to look up and memorize the e-mail address of the police department's tip line.

So, he was ready when late the next day, soon after he got home from work, the doorbell rang. He listened as the delivery truck went down the block, and sure enough, the doorbell rang again. James glanced to be sure the pad and pencil were ready, and opened the door.

It was a different man, and a different car, but was almost surely the same scam. "Can you help us?" the man said. "We're looking for Alexander Street." The man wore a grey jacket that looked almost like a uniform, but James was sure it wasn't.

"You're off the mark," he said coolly. "What's your name?"

The man appeared flustered. "Jones," he finally managed. "Sorry to bother you." He backed away, turned, and started down the porch steps.

Taking his phone from his pocket, James snapped a photo of the man getting into the car, then zoomed in for an excellent photo of the license plate just as the car was about to back hastily down the drive. Taking the pad, he jotted a few notes to prompt memory: faded tan, rusted chrome trim; an absolutely ancient four-door sedan, an Oldsmobile – a brand no longer made. Before the car was out of sight down the street, he had sent the photos to the police tipline. Then he phoned.

"This is James Allen," he told the receptionist, "On Edgewood Street. I've just had a visit from the kind of scam that was in the paper yesterday. I've sent a photo of the criminals' car and license number to the tip line, and I have other details. Can you transfer me to someone who's working on this case?"

In a moment he was talking to a detective, who was evidently pleased. "Thank you for the photos; I have them on my screen. How long ago did they leave?"

"Two or three minutes ago. Headed south on Edgewood Street."

"I'm not sure I recognize the make of that car," the detective said.

"You're too young," James said. "It's an Oldsmobile Alero. They stopped making them, I'll bet more than a decade ago."

"Hold a moment, please." James heard the detective call the dispatcher. "Put out a bulletin." He gave a description of the car and the license plate, and then came back on the phone. "With that unusual make and your photos, we ought to be able to nab them. Could you identify the man who came to your door?"

"I think so. You can see I took his picture before he got in the car."

"Sir, you're a remarkable man and an alert citizen," the detective said. "We could have an arresting officer bring them to your house for positive identification, but then they'd know for sure who turned them in and where you live. Might you come to the station?"

"Of course. Phone me when you've caught them. I'm only ten minutes away."

He had barely started telling Susan about his adventure when the phone rang. "We have them," the detective said, "thanks to you. Could you come to the station?"

"You bet." James shortened his explanation to Susan, put on his coat, and was on his way.

The detective was waiting outside the station. "Mr. Allen?" he said through the car window.

"Yes."

"I know you!" he said. "I've seen your car around town. Love your colour scheme! Park over here in the VIP spot, please, and we'll have you identify the car."

James parked, got out, and looked at the car parked next to him. An ancient tan Alero sedan. "That's the one, officer. Not many like it."

"Wonderful!" said the detective, writing something in a notepad. "With no prompting from me. A rock-solid ID. You're a perfect witness. Come into the station, please."

Perfect witness. The phrase lodged itself firmly in James' memory.

He was led to small room with a chair facing a small window looking into a much larger room. There were a dozen people in that room, most seated on plain wooden chairs. James spotted the man who less than an hour ago had been at his door. He shrank from the window.

"No need to duck, sir. It's a one-way mirror," said the detective. "Did you think you recognized someone?"

"Yes," said James, but was interrupted by a knock on the door.

The detective let a young man into the room. "Mr. Allen," he said, "this is Buddy Goddard from the newspaper. If you don't mind, he'd like to observe, and probably write a news story. We need to encourage more residents to be as organized and observant as you."

"No problem," said James, and paused as his mind searched for better wording. "Anything I can do to help the police do their job," he said. "The public interest is my interest."

"Thank you, sir," said the reporter. He scribbled something in a notebook.

"Come back to the window, sir," the detective said. "Can you see..."

"Unless he's left the room," James interrupted, "he's in there." He sat down on the chair and peered through the little window. "There! The man on the left, standing by the wall."

The detective leaned over James' shoulder. "Tall fellow, grey slacks, grey jacket almost like a uniform?"

"That's the one. Let me just double-check." He took out his phone and thumbed through to the photo he'd taken. "Absolutely," he said. "Not the world's greatest picture, but enough to be sure my memory is correct."

"Good man!" said the detective. "Let's go into a more comfortable room."

"Can you wait just a minute?" the reporter said to the detective. "My photographer has arrived." He turned to James. "I'd like to get a picture of you peering through that one-way window," he said, "if you don't mind."

EXTRAORDINARY

"Glad to be of help," James said. He'd waited a long time for recognition; a few minutes more was nothing.

Within moments someone else appeared in the doorway. A young woman and a burly man with a video camera on his shoulder. "Susan Scranton from Channel Three," said the woman. "We'd like to shoot you making the ID through the window."

The newspaper photographer and the television cameraman obviously knew each other. They worked together to stage a picture of James seated, looking through the window, with the detective over his shoulder. "Can you just point to the culprit, sir?" said the TV fellow.

They had him stay at the window while they moved around the little room to get different angles and had him point through the window twice more. James complied patiently, all the while thinking what Susan would say when he told her all this. Maybe he shouldn't tell; just have her watch the Channel 3 news with him tonight and surprise her.

"Enough!" the detective said at last. "Let's get this good man into a comfortable chair, and you can do your interview." He led them out to a larger room, and stood with an arm around James' shoulders, waiting as the cameras were pointed at them. "This man is a model citizen," he said. "If every resident of the city were as thoughtful and observant, we could wipe out most of these minor crimes."

The reporters wanted to ask a few questions. "Why don't you sit in that comfortable chair? Can I get you a cup of coffee?"

James looked at the offered chair and sensed he would look small and slouched sitting there. "I'll opt for that one," he said, pointing to a hard-backed chair. "And thanks, but I'll wait to have coffee when I get home." He sat and turned to the reporters. "Can I answer any questions?"

"Thank you, sir," said Buddy, the newspaper reporter. "First, can we be sure we have your name right?"

"James Allen," he said. "That's A-double-L-E-N. James Allen." He watched them write in their notebooks. "Not for publication, please, but my *special* friends," he added in a tone meant to include them, "call me Jim."

TIDES

By Claire O'Brien

1994

When I was three years old, I learned to swim by jumping through a hula hoop into the deep end of the Churchfield swimming pool. That's all I remember. The hula hoop and the jump. The next thing I remember is knowing how to swim.

1995 - 2004

As a young girl I craved to be submerged in water, especially open water. Once the water was all around me and I was a part of it, I just needed to keep moving and the cold began to feel like its own safe shelter. The natural world protecting me.

*

Ballybunion beach is one of my favourite places to be. Wading into the sea I scream and shriek with the cold, and with excitement. The water rippling around my belly is the hardest part, the sting of the cold meeting the warm blaze of my middle. My breath comes in short gasps, and then comes the choice whether to go fully in, or not. Looking back now I cannot think of a single time I turned back. I always closed my eyes and sank my body in.

2001

We practise diving in swimming class. We go to the deep end and the teacher holds a long pole in the water in case we are drowning and need to catch it.

*

My Dad tells me that when he was younger, he had a terrible fear of water. He did once overcome this and learn to swim, but then he got out of the habit of it and his fear of water came back. I wish he would relearn to swim, learn to float, and learn to let go of the whole weight of everything.

Mom can swim a little but not confidently. She never had lessons. She tried teaching herself in the sea at Ballybunion when she was a little girl. She has tried to teach herself over the years since. She says she is proud of me that I can swim.

2002

I am eleven or twelve and we are starting to learn about periods in school. I have lots of questions that I never ask. I want to ask somebody "will I feel the blood coming?" but I am too embarrassed. Rumours and horror stories spread around the school of girls walking out of the bathrooms with blood pouring down their legs. I am terrified that will happen to me.

While waiting for my periods to start, I imagine everything is the start of it. There is a wooden rocking chair in my Grandad's house, and it has red crayon, or something stuck on it. Not realising, I sit on it one day with my cream corduroy pants and start to rock back and forth. Afterwards I am left with a thin line of red on the seat of my pants, and even though I quickly realise it isn't blood, it feels like a warning. "Stay vigilant and don't get too sure of yourself. There is a tide coming that will sweep you out to sea. The tide will be red and hot, shameful and unclean."

I still believe my period will be foreshadowed by something, like those red streaks on my pants. Or like the blood from my thumb when I cut it peeling potatoes for Christmas dinner. Our yearly ritual is to prepare the vegetables and potatoes the night before Christmas, as well as melting and setting the jelly for the trifle. In the dimmed light of the kitchen, I stand peeling potatoes, in between putting full cubes of the undiluted jelly in my mouth when no one is looking. Suddenly, I feel the sharp sting of the blade on my skin and go running up the stairs to the bathroom when I see the red blood pour from my thumb.

"Don't forget".

"Stay vigilant".

*

I watched Dad cry today. His tears fell continuously, unyielding and unrelenting. Unstoppable, unbearable. I am only a child. I have not enough life lived to comfort him. I will his eyelids to cloak and cover his shining, mottled green and hazel eyes, to protect their tender viscous fleshy substance. I will him to be at peace.

*

While trying to do a tumble turn in swimming class today, I get stuck halfway. It is the first time I feel afraid in water. I don't know whether to try to reverse my movement or to try to follow through with the turn. I lose all momentum and I am frozen in fear. Imagine if I drown because I can't decide what to do.

2004
In the end, or rather the first time I get my period, I don't feel anything, and nor is it foreshadowed, I simply come home from school one day and go to the bathroom to find a round stain of blood on my underwear.

I call Mom into my bedroom. She takes a clean pair of knickers out of my underwear drawer and holds them so that the gusset part is facing up on her palm. She shows me how to open the sanitary pad and stick it to the material. Saying that for now this will be the easiest way to do it.

*

In the evening I sing in a talent show in school. I return to school after dinner, my first sanitary pad stuck to my underwear, held between my gangly legs. I wear a black dress, with a gold poncho that has intricate designs of flowers made of lace on it. I wear a choker around my neck that makes it harder to breathe and harder to sing. As I sit waiting to go on stage, an older boy I fancy says I am looking good. When I come home and look at myself in the mirror, I see that my ghost white legs are covered in dark hair which I never seemed to have noticed before. I realise the boy I fancied had probably been teasing me. I feel horribly embarrassed.

2004-2010

Every day in school I fear my blood will flow from between my legs onto my grey school skirt, and onto the plastic school chairs. I imagine slipping in a pool of my own blood in the crowded corridors. I don't know when the blood will come, or how much of it there will be. I feel I am sailing the oceans without any knowledge of the tides. I will be caught off guard with every swell and storm. In the toilets I worry other girls can hear me pulling the pad from my underwear, the swift sound of the adhesive being pulled away from the cotton, and I feel ashamed that this is happening to me.

2004

The first day of my period each month the blood flow starts off light and manageable, but during the night I start to bleed profusely. I wake up with the blood having soaked through my pyjamas, through the bed sheets, the mattress protector, and onto the mattress. A pool of blood penetrates through every layer of the bed. I cry in distress, feeling totally alone. I can't leave the house because I am out of pads, and I am afraid to even ask my sister to buy some for me. I have heard Mom call them "s.t's". So, I write a shopping list and hand it to my sister saying there are things Mom has asked us to get for the house. She agrees but as she is leaving she starts to read the list that says "milk, bread, s.t's". She turns around to ask what "s.t's" are. I try to close the front door on her foot, but I can't, and I have to tell her that "s.ts" stands for sanitary towels.

2005

What was once the most carefree part of my life was now also marred with these fears: what if I get my period while swimming and as I walk out of the ocean, with my face ruddy, my lips salty, and my skin covered in goose pimples, there would be blood pouring down my legs and I would be terribly ashamed.

*

I remember walking the beach that summer, the first after the arrival of my periods, looking enviously, and almost angrily at the water. It somehow felt like the water and the natural world had betrayed me. Before, I could

74 CREATIVE NONFICTION

be a part of it anytime I wanted, now, there was an obstacle between me and the sea. A messy and painful thing that kept me at a distance from one of my favourite places, that kept me at odds with that world of freedom, with that world that protected me.

*

I am lying on my side in my bed. The cramps in my stomach have me pulling my knees up to my chest and pressing my fingers to my lips as I try to fall asleep. For a second I cannot speak, then I am whispering mantras.
 "Breathe. Breathe. Breathe."
 "Don't forget."
 "Stay vigilant."

2006

I go to west Cork with A. Thankfully I don't have my period and we go swimming.
 When I lie on my back in the water my lungs, full of fresh air, help me stay afloat.
 Back at the house, as I get changed, I study my adolescent body. I see my body is full of unfilled parts. There are two dimples in the small of my back. They are caused by short cords tethering my pelvis to my skin. When I lie on my side in bed there is a space between my hip and my stomach, as gravity lets the flesh fall away from the bone. There is a dip where my clavicle meets my throat. I push my fingers against the hollow and feel the pressure on my windpipe. For a second I cannot breathe.

2017

It is my birthday and N. and I go to Kinsale. I am on my period but it's light enough to just use my mooncup. I try to impress N. by swimming out as far as the pontoon. On the way out I feel great, but when I reach the floating platform and turn to look back at the shore, I feel scared I have come out too far. I start to swim back, trying to speedily diminish the distance between my body and the sand, pretending I'm not panicking. I make it back and it has the desired effect of impressing N.

2018

I didn't feel my body was my own until now, in my late twenties. I have grown used to how it likes to change, bleed and ache. I can even predict these events with a certain amount of accuracy.

As a child my body was something I gave little thought to, until my stomach ached, or my ankle twisted. I ran almost everywhere and I gave little consideration to the muscles and bones that allowed me to move so joyfully and so freely.

2020

I go to the doctor for the morning after pill, but it has been a few days and she says it won't be effective. I am worried and excited that N. and I might have a baby. We don't, but while searching online for early signs of pregnancy I learn more about my body.

I learn that the womb is a hollow organ. I think of my womb with its lining thickening each month and shedding each month, too. I think of all it could hold and I wonder if it ever will. I think of all of the pain my womb has already caused me and millions of others.

I learn that the heart, too, is hollow. It holds a space for love, like blood to pulse in and out of its chambers. I imagine a heart like a crevice between two rocks, where the tide comes and water rushes in, before being dragged gently back out to sea. My blood, always travelling; the tides, always moving; and love, always changing.

I learn that even though the centre black pupil of our eyes is a hole, water doesn't rush in to fill the gap when we go swimming. I imagine what it might feel like if it did. Like crying in reverse, salty tears flooding into my eyes as I sink my body into the sea. The stinging sensation and being unable to see: the ocean overwhelming my body's defences and pulling me down. Strangely, I also sense a glimmer of peace in that idea. Maybe the water would replenish all of the tears I have cried, and I would be replete. Maybe I would return to a newborn state before any tears had been shed. Maybe I would float, clasping my knees to my chest with both hands, and feel completely protected by the water surrounding me.

2022

Maybe because I am naturally quite quiet or maybe because there was always a lot of talking and arguing at home, I often think I don't have anything to say, until someone is really listening and then, I find I have so much to say, and so many stories to tell that I could easily drown in them. Getting the opportunity to write them down, to carve them into something discreet and hopefully beautiful changes things. Crafting my memories into stories alters my relationship to the brackish water so that instead of drowning in it I might be able to float on its surface and let go of the whole weight of me.

*

I am swimming above miles of water. I cannot see or touch the bottom with my feet. I am treading water, feeling my legs move through the depth of it. My limbs are waving back and forth like seaweed being moved by the tide. I love how the deeper water holds me up and allows me to move more freely. I love that I need to keep moving my arms and legs in order to stay afloat. I love the challenge and the slight danger of it. It would only take a cramp in my foot to incapacitate me. I know you are supposed to lie on your back in that instance but in the panic of that moment would I have the capacity to do that? The world is bottomless. No one has swum this far out before. The lifeguard blows his whistle and beckons me to come in, but I ignore him. He does not understand who I am when I am in the water. He does not know that I am safe here.

THE CROWD

By Robert Coakley

The summer was nearing an end. After another week's work on the farm, David parked the jeep in the field and jumped down into the long grass. He stood awhile, searching the mottled sky for signs of change. The dying sun held some heat, and great swathes of orange stretched across the horizon. The blaze seemed impenetrable. His phone pinged then, and he fished it from his breast pocket. The messages onscreen read,

Molly: Hopefully not anyways.

Molly: I can see it tbh. You're more of a gatherer than a hunter

Molly: Can we expect the heir of bargy castle later on?

David locked the phone and slipped it into the square on his chest. Lazily, he placed a cigarette between his lips and rolled his shirtsleeves over his elbows.

The plumes of smoke rose slowly in the evening air. Like a mourner, David watched their slow procession until they faded out of sight. Flicking away the butt, he walked around to the boot, eased open the doors, and climbed into the darkness. Empty buckets and grain sacks littered the floor. An oil can lay on its side, the fumes mixing with the sweet smell of oats. He pulled a brand-new length of rope from beneath a spare tyre and tested the strength. The nylon felt slick. He coiled the rope neatly and hung the bundle from a nail driven into the wall of the jeep. From behind the driver's seat, he found an empty Quality Street box and shuffled back out into the fresh air. Slamming the doors, he set off strolling across the pasture.

Unperturbed by the man picking mushrooms, cattle moved around him. They huffed and chewed and flicked at flies with their tails. The fragrance of manure was sharp and rose with the heat of the feeding herd. Chuck to chuck, two strays were lined up at the trough by the fence, licking at the green water.

David worked with vigour, idly inspecting the uneaten mushrooms before tossing them into the box or casting them aside for the crows. The black shapes watched from the trees.

His movements were supple, and the shirt grew damp on his back. Flicking away the cigarette, he left the box down beside a clump of hairy thistles. With one fell swoop, he pulled the shirt over his head and knotted the sleeves tight around his waist. Sweat clung to his skin, cooling as the evening air alighted.

Beyond the drone of a faraway tractor, a skein of geese flew into earshot. He searched the sky and took his phone from his pocket. Steadily, the birds came into view, their honking rising as they neared. Cattle looked up from their chewing. David spoke calm words in their direction, and they studied him with curiosity before returning to their grazing.

Wingbeats in harmony, the geese flew overhead. He videoed them in their v-formation, tracking them across the sky. The commotion soon faded, and calmness settled once again. David saved the clip to his camera roll and sent it to Molly with the caption,

serious argument underway here.

With the traces of a smile, he re-watched the video and, putting the phone away, set off foraging again.

Reaching the shade of a lonely hawthorn, David dropped the box and lit another cigarette. The cattle had stopped shadowing him. Across the field they huddled together in a receding patch of sunshine, seldom raising their heads from feeding. Smoking, David walked along the edge of the shade cast by the tree. The white flowers were stained by the sunset's glow. When he finished the cigarette, he stubbed the butt on his palm and tucked it into his arse pocket.

The air was much cooler below the canopy of thorny branches. Placing his palms on the trunk, he felt the chill of the bark and scraped along the rough skin. The mushrooms at the base looked swollen and neglected. They morphed into one organism as they infected the foot of the hawthorn. David hunkered down and took a photo of the growth. Seen through the screen they looked dead in their limpness. He reached out a finger and touched a soft cap. From the forest beyond the farm a chainsaw throttled. The saw revved and spun and sank into the wood of limbs. David pulled his shirt back down over his head and moved back out into the light.

Strolling back towards the jeep, the cattle flanked him and followed in his footsteps, feeding where they liked. They stopped and stared when David slowed to study their lumbering movements. The light was fading fast. On the outside of the herd, signalled by a low grunting, a bullock mounted a heifer, and the pair stepped forward awkwardly. He watched the slow, fumbling shuffle, scratching the stubble on his throat. Each seemed oblivious to the other, their cows' eyes glazed with tired resignation. The heifer planted her hooves in the turf and let fall a yellow gush of urine which drummed on the dirt below. The bullock slumped back down onto all fours and returned to grazing the clover. David retrieved his phone and took a photo of the two animals. He then opened a thread of text messages. The previous two read,

Kevin: Ya look first thing Monday morning will do

Kevin: John p will be out tomoro to look at those calves.

David forwarded the photo to Kevin and typed a reply.

David: Right, grand. Cattle bulling in the hthorn field.

David: Will see you later for one.

Back on the messaging Home screen, he selected the thread with Molly, deliberated, and typed a reply.

David: I may grace the peasantry with a visit yes

As he counted carefully the numbers of the herd, his phone buzzed in his hand. He unlocked it immediately. Onscreen the messages displayed,

Molly: Aren't we lucky

Molly: Heading to O'Sullivan's now for one of the girl's pre-birthday birthdays, thank god!

Molly: I'll hunt you down at the Elf later on though.

David replied with a thumbs-up emoji and pocketed the phone.

Driving back down the laneway, the herd of cattle cantered along the fence-line beside the jeep. They laboured to keep up, and one by one they fell away to return to their ceaseless chewing. Across the gloaming, under the shaded cover of the hawthorn, a bullock stood scratching his flank off the trunk. The white of his mucky underbelly was just about visible against the bark.

*

Later that night, guided by the light on his phone, David strolled down to The Merry Elf pub. The yellow porch lights were beacons in the gloom and slowly, they drew him in.

Inside the door of the pub, a wave of heat from the open fire met him. He shucked off his coat and added it to the pile on the barstool in the corner. The place was packed. David stood searching the throng of bodies for a face he could bear listening to. A close smell of smoke and sweat circled around the low room. Punters roared and laughed and clinked glasses. Any trace of music drowned beneath the wave of voices. David unlocked his phone, scrolled aimlessly, then locked it again. In the black screen he glimpsed a reflection of his eyes glistening wet from the fire and fought a sudden urge to throw the thing at the nearest wall. An elderly man shoved by. As he passed, he looked up into David's face, the tongue caught between the lips, and leaned in close.

"Watch now," he said. "Don't fall into that phone. You might get stuck there."

David laughed and nodded his thanks.

"Good man," he said. "At least I have someone looking out for me."

The words were swallowed by the din. David watched him shuffle on without reply. Raising his porter to the ceiling, the old farmer locked arms with a young woman wearing bangles on her wrists and, to an uproar of stomps and whistles, the pair spun round and round.

His hands in his pockets, David squeezed his way through to the bar. Shoulder to shoulder, a row of wolf-eyed men sat slurping pints and shouting between sips. He ordered a pint and glanced at the faces on the stools. Nods were shared, and David tried to relax into the spot he'd carved out for himself. As he waited, he felt sweat pooling under his armpits and wafted his shirt.

High up on a shelf behind the bar a stuffed pheasant with one glass eye and a sad array of colours stood watching him. A layer of dust lay thick across the head, dulling the shine of the emerald feathers. David retrieved his phone to take a photo and, catching the curious stares of familiar faces in the mirror behind the bar, scrolled through his messages instead.

A pint of Guinness landed on the counter. As he went to pay the barman, David dropped the coins and scrambled to catch the strays. A twenty-cent coin hopped on the bar and rolled over the edge. It seemed to hang in the air for an age before landing tails down on the grimy boards below. The money rescued and safely handed over, David said a few words about the local GAA club and took a gulp of porter.

"The lads miss you something fierce anyways," the barman said.

David's phone pinged, and he ignored the barman's comment. The screen displayed,

Kevin: Not tonight boss.

With his phone in one hand and the pint in the other, he pushed his way back towards the door. Crossing the dancefloor, a bare-chested fella with his shirt knotted around his waist stumbled backwards and knocked into David. He managed to save the pint, but a glob of porter fell to the floor, splattering his shoes. The man swivelled round, the eyes floating, the cheeks damp and rosy, and blubbered his sorrys. David nodded and made for the door.

Outside, the air was sharp. There was also a great stillness. He checked his emails, his socials, then scrolled through the memories in his camera roll. Lost in the screen, David fished out a cigarette and sparked a lighter. Muffled conversation and the sporadic strum of a fiddle could be heard from inside the pub. He opened the messaging thread with Molly and read through his replies from the last few weeks since they met online. As he smiled or shook his head, he wandered away from the floodlight over the porch and stood by the road.

Somewhere beyond the village the vague loops of a distant siren sounded. Casually, David looked up from the screen. The siren dropped off and came again stronger, rising and fading in the thin air. In a window of the pub the punters carried on their ceaseless conversation. He studied their animated expressions, the way they squealed and creased and contorted their faces into happiness. The barman's practiced smile arrived at a window. He fidgeted with the cords, peering out into the night. David held up his pint in salute, and one by one the blinds came down. The dark figure of his reflection surfaced on the glass again. He searched the shape for likeness and found only unkeen features obscured by distance. The siren's shrill pulled his gaze to the skies. Reflected in the moonlit clouds, David spotted the first flickers of the neon lights and opened the camera on his phone.

After what seemed like a lifetime of waiting, a squad car emerged from a tunnel of oaks arching over the road and tore along towards the pub. Dazzled by the headlights, David stepped away from the edge and started recording. They sped past The Merry Elf in a blaze of blue lights, spitting up stones in their wake. He videoed them as the car shrank into the darkness and disappeared finally out of sight. Though the tailwind had set rustling the low branches of the trees, the road was once again quiet. He stood awhile and, listening to the siren's slow recession into nothing, watched the spot where the lights had vanished. Catching himself, he saved the video and sent it to Molly with the caption.

Busy night ahead.

The door of the pub flung open then, and a swarm of bodies stumbled out into the courtyard. The heat followed them, fading into the night as plumes of white breath. They continued their shouting, drunk and giddy on the excitement of a scandal. Absently fingering a shaving-cut under his chin, David watched them. A speck of blood came away on his fingertip. He downed the dregs of his pint and let the glass fall to the ground where it bounced once and shattered on the second landing. Besides the few side-eyeing stragglers, the locals ignored David and speculated about the siren, roaring at the comical suggestions.

Overhead the clouds looked solid and unchangeable. David stood searching the grey mass for some sign of colour. His phone rang then. Without checking the caller, he planted his boots and flung the thing over a ditch, where it landed face down in a shallow gully. An uproar of laughter started. David swivelled round, the eyes wet with tears, a white frothing showing in the corners of the mouth, and watched a few punters file back into the pub. Through the open door the fiddle and the low lilt of a ballad escaped. David turned from the music, crunching broken glass beneath his boots. Someone called his name. A familiar voice, the tone of care. They pleaded through the darkness, their desperation mounting as David slipped silently away from the crowd and disappeared into the tunnel of oaks arching over the road.

ANTS FROM UP HERE

By Cian Dunne

Aged three, Isaac is obsessed with tiny things. Especially insects, the tiniest things he knows to exist. Ladybirds scuttle across his hairless hands. Blood-sucking spots of red move him from the wall to the grass. Obsession does not eliminate the taste to hurt them. Slap, stomp, swat. Spiders get the worst of it. That's what they get for appearing in his shower while he scrubs himself clean. With his wet foot they'll be swept to swirl down the drain with the water, brown from his muddy knees.

Once, lifting up a loose stone, there were hundreds of ants hiding beneath, scurrying around amongst each other. He lifted the stone beside it. Hundreds more. They separated from the centre but still managed to stick together. It reminded him of standing in the middle of the school playground while the other kids swarmed around him. From then on, ants had held his attention and his affections.

One day, Isaac takes a magnifying glass from a drawer at home, wipes it clean. With this, he can make the ants look big, and suddenly small again. It is all up to him, all down to him.

Aged five, Isaac has his first real problems at school. Trouble seeing the teacher's writings on the whiteboard. His parents drag him in by the ear for an eye test. The people are nice to him only because they stand to make a fortune from his inability to see things as they are. They spend an hour deciding which frames will be his first. He looks at himself in the mirror, doesn't see himself in the reflection. Only the glasses. He practises wearing them around the house for the rest of the weekend. Monday morning at school, they don't come out of the case that came with them.

When Isaac is six, his gaze goes up. To the little lights in the sky, so many of them, that denote the stars. His dreams go to rest up there in their sparks. Hopes, big ones and little ones. The ones he'll say out loud and the ones he'll keep in his head. His parents knock on his bedroom door to no response. Open it, give it a performative knock. Watch him from the door but he is dead to the world, sight, and mind elsewhere, way beyond his room, their imagination. While he stares at the stars they stare at each other, then leave and shut the door behind them. The next day they buy him a telescope to indulge his new interest. It's set up, stationed at his bedroom window, set at a slant with the roof. Just like the ants, now he can see the stars bigger than they are. Really, though, he knows he sees them smaller than they *really* are. Shapes he sees too. Orion and Cassiopeia, on separate nights. Several times, shooting stars fly across the lens. He cannot catch them, but they've been captured. In the eye of his mind.

Aged seven, Isaac's feet leave the ground for the first time. On the plane over, so scared by the sounds, he falls asleep. He wakes up in a different country. On the fifth day, they go on a drive through the Bavarian Alps. At a standstill, with borrowed binoculars he sees Austria all the way from Germany. He cannot tell the subtle differences between them.

Too soon, they're on the plane back. A mix up with the seating means that he sits separately from his folks. Him in the aisle seat, his feet don't touch the carpet surface. To his left, an adult man sits in the window seat. The size of him frightens Isaac – he almost takes up the seat between them, too. It's evening outside, brightness darkening. Ascending, the adult turns to him. This brute is just a bigger child.

"Look," the big child says, pointing down to the earth. "They look like ants from up here."

When they touch down, it is dark.

His parents tuck him into bed, and he gets two kisses in quick succession, both above the eyes.

"Why the long face?"

"We went up, but it got too dark to see the stars up close. And when we were going down, I missed you."

WAYWARD SUN

By Isa Robertson

The boy wanted only one thing: to reach the sun. This was his life's work. To him, it seemed a long journey, but not impossible. He did not know when he would arrive, but he hoped it would be before he died.

Every morning, when the sun broke over the mountains, he set out for it. He walked with a stick, since often his quest took him over land that was slow and difficult to travel.

By noon, he would have nearly reached the sun. It was almost overhead. He thought that when it came right overhead, he would climb up a tree to close the final distance. He had seen that the sun sometimes touched the tops of the trees. He would climb one, and when the sun touched it, he would grab on to the sun and let go of the tree.

But he never reached a tree directly under the sun that he could climb. The sun was always just off to one side — or he was. So, he would run in order to get under the sun and start climbing. But the sun ran, too, toward the mountains on the other side of the valley. He would walk all evening after it, without catching up, and then it would hide behind the mountains.

Patiently, he would wait for it.

Then it would surprise him and appear from behind mountains that were not the ones it had hidden behind. He did not understand why, but it did not matter. When it reappeared, he started walking toward it, full of hope.

The villagers called him simple, or worse. Some said his mother must have eaten the wrong kind of root; some said that he must have been dropped when he was a baby. He had never spoken, though he listened intently. All manner of cures were attempted. None worked, and at last he was allowed to do the thing that he wanted to do the most: follow the sun.

The villagers — rather, his mother — fed him, and kept an eye on him. His pace did not change, so it was rarely difficult to guess where he would be at a given time, if you needed to find him: he would be somewhere near where he had been at that time of day yesterday ... and the day before ... and the day before that.

Eventually, the boy's grandfather came to visit. He lived far, far away, and was always busy. He had not made the journey to the village since the boy was a baby. But even so, the villagers had heard tales of his great store of knowledge, and his great wisdom. Some claimed that the boy's grandfather, who was only a priest, was smarter than the king, and could beat anyone who challenged him to games of the mind. When he arrived in the village, he was treated with respect, despite his grandson's strangeness, and nobody challenged him to games.

He went to his daughter's house. The boy's mother, when he asked, told him about the boy, and his pursuit of the sun. The next day the grandfather set out to meet the boy, just as his route would take him close to the village.

When the boy came into view, the grandfather just watched. If the boy knew who he was, he did not show it. The boy looked up at the sun and made his way toward it.

The grandfather approached, and the two looked at each other. After a time, the grandfather said, "May I walk with you?"

The boy moved his head up and down slightly.

The grandfather fell into step, and they both followed the sun until it hid behind the mountains.

The next day word reached the village that the grandfather had joined the boy on his circular pilgrimage. Some went to see it with their own eyes, in case they were being told tall tales. They were not.

Always before they had laughed. They watched the two, and this time they did not laugh. This old priest was said to be stuffed with learning until you couldn't fit any more books in. If he thought this walking toward the sun was worth doing, it could not be a joke. It must be something else, something that only he understood.

Now that they had stopped laughing at the boy, they noticed something about the expression on his face. They all noticed it, but they had trouble saying what it was that they all noticed. So, they just said, see the expression on his face? And they said, yes, yes, I see.

It glowed like the sun it was turned towards. And the glow seemed to be spreading to the grandfather's face.

WAYWARD SUN

The mother brought two meals the next day.

At dawn, they set out again. They walked, as always, in silence.

"Grandfather," the boy said, "are we getting closer?" His voice sounded old from disuse.

The grandfather nodded.

FAR SIDE OF THE MOON

By Colm Brennan

Before I knew anything of time that didn't belong to only me, I sometimes sat and watched spiral galaxies in my coffee cup. The formation of stars and planets from elemental dust in the swirling foam of freeze-dried Nescafé. Gravity, centrifugal force, tiny bubbles hurtling around one another, falling toward the centre. Drawn together but also pulling apart. The entire universe. Infinite lifetimes.

Then I got used to using the quieter moments to attempt to think of nothing at all. Quiet became its own end. Space but with room for little else.

Before I knew anything of babies crying, I used to wonder what it was like for Apollo 11's Command Module Pilot, Michael Collins, the farthest man from earth. When Aldrin and Armstrong were on the lunar surface, he spent almost an hour of each orbit without radio contact. Alone on the other side of the moon, immersed in an absence of everything he thought he knew. Was he able to savour the tranquillity when moments before there had been chaos?

Chaos like a baby crying.

Their cries are specifically designed to infiltrate their parents' nervous systems, target primitive amygdalae, drain depleted levels of serotonin and pump pure adrenalin into that vacuum.

A painting hanging in the hall distracts him. A Haitian mountain village. He's drawn to the texture of the primary colours punched on canvas and reaches out toward the crude shapes depicting powerful women hacking coconuts out of tall trees and crouching to harvest peanuts. And I think my life is hard. I've never climbed a tree with a machete.

Come on, we can't stand here all night. Let's go, before my mind starts to run away with itself.

Luckily, the mirror in the bedroom then steals his attention and brings us closer to our destination. The glass is grubby and smudged from where he bats at his reflection. He is becoming more dexterous, more curious, and he frowns now when his fingertips meet those of the image of another baby. Neurons firing. Synapses lighting like stars in the night sky.

Who is *that* in the mirror?

For his sake, I want to sound astonished, but my chest tightens, and I can feel the muscles around my mouth twitch as fluctuations in my breath cause a wobble in my voice.

'Is that a *baby* in the mirror?'

His identical twin died in the womb and our two boys were born together a month later. Just twenty-seven weeks gestation.

First out, arrived crying.

If you know anything about preterm babies, you will understand what a remarkable, joyous statement that is. Functional, fully formed lungs that had only 194 days to mature but with enough strength to force breath over tiny vocal cords and proclaim his arrival by projecting definite, unambiguous acoustic waves that rang out to cheers of celebration in the delivery room. His brother followed, quiet, as we knew he would be, peaceful and still. His, destined to be a distinctive and ethereal presence in our lives. So, moments like this at the mirror can catch me off guard. Especially at night. Because it's getting more difficult to imagine two in this world. It's also confusing. I say distinctive and ethereal but more often than not it's a challenge to locate his presence and I find myself wondering where exactly is my son? The baby has stopped crying. He's fresh, as if he'd just slept twelve hours. He reaches out, gets some fingers up my nose, the other hand pulls my bottom lip. He is, of course, oblivious to this question for now, and most of time his budding personality, which is already evolving and growing in complexity, distracts me from it too. Five months corrected is eight months (chronologically), but it's as if he always existed. You could almost be forgiven for believing the human soul is somehow separate from the transience of life on earth. Almost. The mirror plays a cruel trick. They may have looked alike, but both possessed individuality impossible to duplicate.

You might wonder where their mother is. She's beside me. Through everything. My wife has suffered and suffers still and all that we have endured has been refracted through her own unique prism. It's not my place to attempt to put words on it. She might, one day, or she might not paint or sculpt or stretch or sew it into being. I hope she does. I can only reveal my experience, layered under pseudoscientific-tinged musings, which, I might add, she doesn't recognise. She's read this and feels quite separate from it. I suppose, consciousness gives us versions that are particular to ourselves and no one else. No wonder the world finds it so hard to agree with itself.

When sleep does decide to visit the baby, it's with the unexpectedness of a new moon. Sharp, delicate, fleeting. He goes down and then I lie on the bed. The quiet is as loud as the baby was moments ago and I begin to wonder about all that other stuff again, except this time with some experience to colour it and let me tell you, the far side is nothing like I imagined. The problem is, I can't stay awake at night for very long. Once horizontal, my eyes close like one of those creepy dolls with weighted eyelids. That said, I have come to identify a moment before unconsciousness, before dreaming, that seems to envelope everything. It's a glimpse of infinity. It happens when the senses stop trying to do their job and everything isn't filtered through logic for a change.

So, now, as I write this, not in bed, sleep deprived, but at my desk nearly 18 months later, with a toddler in the other room and my wonderful wife lying on the couch, pregnant again, I wonder if *that* (the infinite space before sleep) is where I can find him. My missing son. It's a reassuring thought because I go there often, after all, at least once a day.

So, my boy, if you're out there (apologies to the reader who has accompanied me this far, but I've just realised that this is no longer for you), before I fall fully asleep, that is where I'll meet you. And together we can float in our own temporary abyss.

BENVOLIO'S SECRET

By Valerie Hunter

Mrs. Sheehan urges the class to notice details when they read, so Kieran tries his best. *Romeo and Juliet* is not his favorite — the endless angst, the histrionics, the lust – but he likes that some of the characters call Romeo out on his ridiculousness, even if Romeo never listens. And he particularly likes Benvolio, so calm, so practical.

He hones in on one of Benvolio's lines in act one: "A troubled mind drave me to walk abroad." Of course, no one bothers asking Benvolio what his troubles are, but Kieran wants to ask, wants to imagine that Benvolio is like him, that he's taking those troubled morning walks because they're a break from pretending to be a 'normal' boy, all that excruciating pressure to find a girl and get down to business. Maybe, when Benvolio listens to Romeo whine on and on about Rosaline, he just wants to say, "Who really cares, mate? Your problem is so pedestrian compared to mine; you'll find another girl, and everything will work out for you (as long as she's not a Capulet)."

Kieran clings to this thread of kinship, disappointed when Benvolio disappears midway through the play, no longer needed. At least he doesn't die, which can surely be considered an accomplishment in a Shakespearean tragedy.

Did they even have a word for asexual back then? Probably not. Supposedly Shakespeare was bi, and judging by the endless innuendo in his plays, sex was on his mind a lot. Maybe he never even realized that some people didn't feel the urge, or, if he did, maybe he thought it was unnatural, perverse. Still, Mrs. Sheehan says Shakespeare frequently subverted expectations, as well as being an innovative wordsmith, so Kieran thinks he could have come up with some turn of phrase to capture it, preferably something magical rather than offensive.

When they finally finish reading and the stupid feud has ended, Mrs. Sheehan asks them to write a story from a secondary character's perspective revealing a secret they held. His classmates grumble, but Kieran returns to Benvolio's "troubled mind" line, composes a whole monologue where Benvolio explains who he really is to Romeo, and Romeo actually gets his head out of his arse long enough to listen and be kind.

In the end, though, Kieran hands in a tale in which Benvolio is having a secret affair with Rosaline, how they're madly in love and afraid Romeo will find out. Mrs. Sheehan gives him an A and praises his creativity, and Kieran smiles and keeps Benvolio's secret to himself.

THE HUNGRY BOG

By Robert Coakley

Clonycavan Man,
Somewhere between the ancient kingdoms of Brega & Mide,
Ballivor,
Clonycavan,
Co. Meath.

Early Iron Age, 392-201 BC.

Bog Bodies Research Project,
National Museum of Ireland – Archaeology,
Kildare St, Dublin 2.

Dear Sir/Madam,

I hereby donate my future bog body to science, and consent to the Bog Bodies Research Project completing the following scientific analyses on what's left of me:

+ Anatomical, pathological, pollen, isotopic, dental, and dietary analysis
+ Fingerprinting
+ Physical reconstruction
+ Graphic recording
+ DNA assessment
+ Histological analysis of tissue samples
+ Dermatological analysis of skin samples
+ Gut and stomach content analysis
+ Identification of parasites (internal & external)

CREATIVE NONFICTION

- Radiocarbon dating
- CT scanning
- MRI scanning
- Infrared and ultraviolet photography.

I hope this finds you well.

Respectfully,
Clonycavan Man.

P.S. An air-conditioned, spot-lit, raised glass coffin will do the trick.

Inside the National Museum of Ireland – Archaeology, at the 'Kingship & Sacrifice' exhibition. A hall sunk in shadows and solemnity. Writing this letter on the inside of your skull, you imagine *An Post* bollixed up and delivered it to someone's granny out in Bally-go-backwards, and not to the head honchos of the Bog Bodies Research Project. They have about as much consent to exhibit these corpses as the buckos who tied Oldcroghan Man to the basement of the bog pool out Offaly ways. To secure him in his grave, they shoved twisted hazel ropes, coined withies, through cuts in the cratur's arms as if he was a tent needing pegging. A defence wound on one arm is evidence enough of noncompliance.

Stumbling across this exhibition, your curiosity concerning an afterlife and how humans' journey there germinates. You find yourself examining your experiences with death and burial as a lapsed catholic, inspecting one particular loss in depth, comparing a friend's tragic inhumation to that of the Bog Bodies and their unearthing, their surfacing. Though lacking in consent, this exhibition tells the story of in-between spaces. It tells the story of the forgotten. The showcased. The unburied.

The three men exhibited – or what's left of them – lie in their respective glass cases: Clonycavan Man, Oldcroghan Man, Gallagh Man. The gloom of the bog stalked them here, surfacing as a lonesome aura. Each man has their own concealed section with a plaque of information offered as a warning – as close as they'll get to an epitaph. You follow the bend of each section to their spot-lit resting places, not unlike an aquarium for corpses.

Standing inches from the Iron Age, a time when human sacrifice for fertility set the standard and crossed fingers had no pull, you get a sense of loitering on sacred ground, a sense of seeing something you shouldn't.

This uneasiness at glimpsing something unnatural sends your thoughts flailing back four years to when you were twenty years old, staring at your friend's lifeless body. A white sheet covered him from toes to chin, unlike the naked bodies being exhibited. A crowd of mourners had gathered outside the house, watching from a distance. Soon he would go into the ground, surrounded by friends and family. But what happened after? When the graveyard emptied, and the sobs subsided? Was his body preserved as it lay before you? Pulled from the earth and placed on display?

The day your friend died started no different to the usual simulation. The fishing village of Kilmore Quay sat on the side-line watching the Irish Sea collide with the Atlantic, an enthralling matchup if you were that way inclined. A breed of surrealism seemed to haunt the place. Hordes of beefed-up birds swooped low squawking, pickpocketing unsuspecting people of battered sausages. Barking, a seal swam the rounds for scraps. Was there a solemn note in the pitch? Fishermen lugged coffins of sea creatures to land, and the Atlantic's tongue licked its wounded shoreline – one piece of plastic at a time.

Working in Lick'd, the ice-cream parlour, you remember the never-ending queue, the faces overflowing with smiles and syrup. Oblivious to the outside world and its cogs clanking, you flung gelato at kids, counting the seconds to salvation. The evening held plans of night swims, after-parties, and alcohol. With spirits high, the minutes dragged, and you felt the pang of time wasted, never to be revived.

Did you miss the first call and catch the second? You don't remember. Details as such sound trivial, but obsessions are inexplicable to the unaffected. Do you consider yourself affected? Not to the same degree as some. You're a son and a brother before you're a friend. Two of your mates mumbled on the other end of the phone, pausing, and starting and stuttering. They took turns trying to convince you of your friend's death. You thought their tears sounded fake. Reeling, you told them to grow up, hung up, and headed back to dish out more sundaes.

Your friends always took the piss – prank calls not the norm, but certainly not unheard of. Mind, this one sat awkwardly with you. A wrench lodged in your chest, turning on some rounded bolt. You slipped outside again and walked up the street, away from the mayhem. You had to ring your friend's father. An excuse about hurling would do the trick.

His father had few words, only confirmation. The timbre of his voice lent itself to a man fighting a losing battle in himself. His cadence has stayed with you, growing stronger with the years, and now a well of strength you return to. Without a word, you hung up and slipped back into the simulation, back through the layers of reality. Delighted parents bustled by, pushing prams and expectations. Screams of delight or demand rung. They searched their children for signs of their future, for signs of who they would become, the occupations awaiting them.

A cushy occupation awaited Oldcroghan Man, but decapitation destroyed his dreams. At the exhibition, you examine him through his showcase. According to his epitaph, carefully manicured fingernails and an absence of wear to his hands indicates a lack of manual labour and a high social rank. Oldcroghan Man's parents had aspirations for their son, no doubt. You wonder did they ever visit his burial site, or crime scene? Did they even know of his death? Holding concrete proof of a son's passing must feel worse than oblivion itself, but the not knowing, the suspicions, and the hope of his return home, seems a lonelier life to live. Regardless of class, they say everyone is equal in death – buried, cremated, or stuck to the bottom of a bog pool. But what of the people they leave behind?

An elderly man saunters into the exhibition, holding a wrist behind his back. You'd like to ask him, what in-the-name-of-Maradona is going on here?

Of course, here being "the time and space between life and death, too late to return to the living and not time, not yet, not for a while, to be quite dead".

But he doesn't hang around; feck all to see here.

Sarah Moss' words stuck like a pebble in your throat, you leave the exhibition and the bog bodies behind. How long will they float between here and there? Dead amongst the living. Another thousand years? Once preserved by natural chemicals in the land they farmed, now pinned to the present by climate-controlled display cases.

After the phone call with your friend's father, yours collected you from the ice-cream parlour. Driving in silence, you headed for your friend's house. Knowing your best friend has passed away and not seeing concrete evidence embodies the space between life and death. Though you heard his father's voice waver with words of confirmation, you held your friend in your heart as living and breathing. You needed to see him to believe it.

What the fuck was he thinking? your father said, gripping the wheel.

He knew you had no answer for him, and still don't. Your lips felt dry. Licking them you tasted the salt of sea air, of tears. You rolled down the window and closed your eyes against the gushing air. Your nose found the changes of terrain. Ocean smells receded. Ploughed fields paraded their soil. Rows of silage sunbathed, and tar bubbled below. You skimmed along the surface of the road towards truth. Towards proof.

Leaving the National Museum of Ireland, you stop at reception for a sconce and confirmation regarding the bog bodies' authenticity. The receptionist, an animated sort, is roaring politely at some fella with limited lingo.

WHAT'S. YOUR. NUMBER? CONTACT. TRACING.

You enquire if the bog bodies are replicas, or what's the story? You're told in no uncertain terms that those are real human beings, like you and me. Leathery looking, but genuine stuff.

You expect a history lesson in return for your curiosity, but instead he shrivels up in himself and goes, the hair and nails? UGH, just disgusting.

Kildare Street with the sun gawking over the rooftops. The late morning whispering of lunch and a black coffee. Walking to the Luas, you think: Jaysus, if he finds those disgusting, wait until he reads their epitaphs. Wait until he hears how they met their end. Was it the Gallagh Man garrotted with the band of willow whips? Flexed by familiar hands, they kept his deerskin cape upon his back, even as he sunk through the layers, through the years. 1821, he rose again like a vacuum-packed Clark Kent – bacteria his kryptonite, stealing away his fermented locks. You wonder if your friend will rise again someday – against his will or otherwise.

CREATIVE NONFICTION

Sitting in his living room all those years ago, a comedy betrayed the circumstances. You few close friends chatted, as if a solution could still be excavated from the ruin. The surreal feeling followed you from the Quay, blunting any feelings you had about the situation. Everything seemed ridiculous. Why were we in that room, in that house, at that time? So many half-baked questions left unanswered. Stoical as ever, his father walked in, putting you at ease from the off. Your friend had the same way about him. You imagined the whole team huddled in the dressing room before a match, shaking with nerves, expecting a trouncing, and in walks your friend. A communal exhale would fill the room.

Would ye like to come in and see him, lads?

You hop off the Luas in Phibsborough. Rather than pointing for home, you follow your legs to Glasnevin Cemetery – The Ritz of Dublin's resting places, where the big fella Michael Collins lies easy beneath speckled marble and lamentations, undisturbed by peat-cutting machines, though not prying eyes. The scenery around Glasnevin Cemetery boasts an intimidating perimeter wall, a smattering of mature trees, a visitor centre, and Ireland's tallest round tower. There's a commercial hopelessness about the place. A two hour drive south, your friend has a more atmospheric setting for his final resting place – not that it matters when you're underground, right?

At the foot of County Wexford lies Our Lady's Island. From up on its perch on the hill, the cemetery at Eardownes Great watches over Lady's Island Lake – a haunt of many rare bird species like the Western Cattle Egret and the Siberian Chiffchaff, not that your friend would give two shites if he saw them.

When you visit your friend's grave, you make sure to call down for sunset when you can watch the pink hues dance on the lake together and track gliding silhouettes across the clouds. The question of whether humans are equal in death puzzles you when you visit Our Lady's Island Cemetery.

After your visit to the exhibition today, you think there must be some significance to where you're buried, or if. You picture the peace of dusk at Eardownes Great. You conjure the lonesome aura of the exhibition on Kildare Street. You listen to Boeings over Glasnevin, and think: bury me somewhere beautiful, and deep down. Too deep to dig out.

The occult aside, you seem to have Glasnevin Cemetery to yourself. You stroll between rows and rows of the dead, reflecting on what it means to go into the soil, to be buried. If you follow Sue Rainsford to the ground, she will show you its healing power, but what of its preservation power?

Weeks after the funeral, you knelt by your friend's grave at Eardownes Great, and thought of Rainsford's advice about the soil, urging him to hear:

"If it takes you there's not much you can do. Try not to squirm and keep one hand straight up in the air. If you go in over your head, try not to open your mouth and eyes. No matter how long you're there for, keep your face shut up tight."

You wonder if similar words were offered to the bog bodies before their descent into the ground. You asked the naked Clonycavan Man for his thoughts, though putting ear to glass, you found his axe-cracked skull empty. Thoughts disappeared in the bog like air from a deflating balloon. Eviscerated, his guts were gone, and you hadn't the stomach to push him for an answer. Unlike those that forced him under the slopping bog water into his pit of peat, his temporary grave, where humic acid pickled his corpse, staining him bronze for centuries. Until a harvester trundled along, scraping at the surface.

The repose of the graveyard ripples. A child's distant wailing. Jackdaws jump and swoop off on a nothing breeze. But sure, weren't they all children really? Clonycavan Man, twenty-five years old at the time of death. Oldcroghan Man the same. Your friend, twenty years old. Youngsters starting out. You borrow Heaney's words for them instead, sharing them softly with the horizontal congregation.

> through my fabrics and skins
> the seeps of winter
> digested me,
> the illiterate roots
>
> pondered and died
> in the cavings
> of stomach and socket

You interrogated his neighbour, Oldcroghan Man, about the fatal blow to his heart. A lover, maybe? Decapitated, he couldn't even meet your eye, let alone discuss his love life. What about those men? Those men, those men, those men that sliced your nipples from your chest and severed your thorax for a finish?

I lay waiting

on the gravel bottom,
my brain darkening,
a jar of spawn
fermenting underground

And the bog. What of the hungry bog?

FEATURED WRITER
INTERVIEW

IN CONVERSATION WITH SUE RAINSFORD

To help any aspiring or emerging writers, we were lucky enough to sit down and get some advice from award-winning writer Sue Rainsford.

Sue Rainsford is an Irish fiction and arts writer based in Dublin. A graduate of Trinity College, IADT, and Bennington College, she is a recipient of the VAI/DCC Art Writing Award, the Arts Council Literature Bursary Award, and a MacDowell Fellowship. She has been awarded residencies by such institutions as the Irish Museum of Modern Art and Maynooth University, and recent commissions include RTÉ Radio 1 and BBC Radio 4. Her début novel, *Follow Me to Ground*, was originally published by New Island Books in Ireland, where it received the Kate O'Brien Award, was long-listed for the Desmond Elliott Prize and the Republic of Consciousness Award when it was published in the UK by Doubleday, and received starred reviews from *Kirkus Reviews* and *Publishers Weekly* when it was released in the US by Scribner. Her short story, "Shorn", was a finalist for the 2021 New York Radio Festival Awards. Most recently, her second novel, *Redder Days*, was published in Ireland and the UK by Doubleday in 2021, and she was appointed Writer in Residence at UCD for 2022.

*

Sinéad: The theme of Issue VII is Identity. In your writing, you reveal various experiences of womanhood through isolation and the body. What does the theme of Identity mean to you and how do you engage with that?

Sue: It's an interesting question because it's quite specific. I don't really approach different projects with a certain question in mind, certainly not fiction. I'm so concerned with embodiment and embodied experiences and forms of knowledge, so identity for me is a compilation of embodied experiences, and what the body accrues over time. As one is moving through the world – things or sensations that you pick up, memories and experiences that you pick up – where do they go inside the body? Where do they go inside flesh?

Someone like Paul B. Preciado would be really important to me in thinking about those things. Even Elena Ferrante writes in terms of flesh being loaded up with ideology, and it makes me wonder how you go into that. How do you put into that or revoke any of that if it's a harmful ideology that she's looking at in very misogynistic and poverty-stricken Naples.

For me, I do think it's very useful to think about big questions and big themes, but when I'm working on a particular piece, I try to distil it all into, "what does one body know on any given day about itself?" And when thinking about something as convoluted and messy as womanhood, if you were to strip back all of culture and ideology and just give a body a fresh start in the world, what does that body come to know about itself? And for the female body – a body that menstruates, for example – what is that experience like for a body that does not have any taboos or culturalisms attached? If you were just to meet your body afresh, in an experience like menstruation, how would that read to you? How would that feed into your sense of self? Identity would very much be a composite of different experiences for me.

Sinéad: What I love in your writing is that, in a similar vein, you connect the mind and the body really well, whereas oftentimes they are disconnected, not just in literature but in life. It's interesting to see you write the abject not just in a bodily way but in a mindful way.

Both *Follow Me to Ground* and *Redder Days* incorporate archetypal horror figures: the mother nature of *Follow Me to Ground*, and the over-reliant twins in *Redder Days*. These are figures you see in so many different mediums. How do you find these ideas? Does your writing start with an image that you expand on, or how do they come to you?

Sue: It starts with an image. Depending on how resonant or how fecund the image strikes me, then I'll know if this image is the root of a short story or a novel or a novella. *Follow Me to Ground* started with this image of a daughter and her father digging a grave for a woman who was not yet dead, and the whole book – the theory, research, other reading – was channelled into that image and what that image afforded me in terms of narrative: why are they digging the grave? How do they know she's going to die? Why are they burying her in their back garden? Why is there a lack of ceremony? And what is the nature of their relationship?

The first image of *Redder Days* was of twins, of a brother and sister, and the idea that you, arguably, cannot be closer to anybody than you are to your own twin, but they are passing each other at dusk and dawn, so while they are incredibly close, there is something slippery or evasive in that closeness.

I am very interested in archetypes and alternative archetypes. Especially when we might think about femininity and how it might be subverted in a positive way – in a way that makes more space for different versions of the feminine. So, with Ada, there was an archetypal virgin girl, although she's not really a girl but is yet distinctly feminine. She's seen as this virginal healer, then she becomes increasingly uncompromising in her desires, and that's where the horrific element in that book comes from for a lot of people: when a female figure no longer acts exclusively in the service of others.

In *Redder Days*, the mother figure was one of my favourite characters to write because she's a problematic mother figure. But why is she problematic? The love that she's giving her children isn't seen to be the right kind of love, or a sufficiently maternal kind of love. It's quite a brooding love. So again, that idea of looking back to archetypes, and being mindful of how they occupy our psyches on a day-to-day basis, and thinking, "if we can wriggle around inside of them and subvert them, what space do they afford us? Within fiction, but also how we are looking at ourselves and people out and about in the world?"

Sinéad: You have such a strong and unique voice in horror, while still using a very minimalist language that could be likened to Samuel Beckett or Eimear McBride. You twist meanings and command how the word is meant to be read. How do these other writers help inform your own voice? How do you take influences and find your own genre within them?

Sue: When *A Girl is a Half-Formed Thing* came out, that blew my head off. I was stunned by that book. I was working on a very early draft of *Follow Me to Ground* at that time. I remember ordering it from Galley Beggar Press, I remember it coming in the post, I remember reading it in the garden. I remember everything about it.

When trying to craft my own style, all I can do as a writer is read and read and read and read and then do *close* readings of the texts. It's something I started doing when I was doing my MFA, but I've started incorporating it into my casual reading life. When I read other authors, I'd break down a sentence clause by clause, phrase by phrase. I'd get really tight and think, "what is that comma doing? What is this semi colon doing? How would the sentence behave if there was a full stop here?" Whenever I'm reading, I always mark in what I would do to the syntax if it were me writing. And I think doing that on a scholastic level during my MFA was a real eye-opener for me as I'd had no real training with writing on a craft level. It was a real eye-opener to look in this minute detail, take a paragraph and take it apart sentence by sentence, clause by clause, getting right down into the bones of it about the effect of every single unit on the page.

Now, when I write, I'll start with something like the images I mentioned earlier. I'll put them down on a page and they'll be too much, and I know they're far too much. They're too gratuitous, or they're too wet and sloppy; there's something in excess about them. And then I'll pare them back down and I'll build them back up. But at the point where I'm building them back up, when I feel like they're starting to be diluted, I'll pare them back a bit, then I'll add a little bit more, then I'll pare them back a bit, until they balance. It's incredibly laborious and not at all an economic way to write.

As a writer, I've never been hugely invested in genre. I'll go into a story or a novel with these images that I'm talking about and eventually the strange or the horrific element will produce itself the more I let the characters talk, the more I let them inhabit the world that they're in. Even when I say, "the world that they're in," I don't go in saying they're in X type of world. I feel no burden of world building. I see the writing as taking place in this room with me here now. I'm not projecting myself anywhere. But eventually, something about the characters or something about the story will produce something strange or other. That will then activate the text for me, get things moving and heighten the stakes. Sometimes I could be working on a piece for months before that element makes itself known.

Sinéad: I find that writers are often told to do a 'what if' exercise where something has happened and let it spiral from there. It's nice to know that you can go with an image that haunts and fascinates you and not exactly know where it's going but play with it in your own way.

Sue: It's a difficult way to write, because you're asking for a lot of trust from the reader and you're also putting a lot of burden on your language. There has to be huge excitement in the language for the ideal reader to stick with you.

Sinéad: When you finished *Follow Me to Ground*, did you feel it was a risk to put it out there knowing that you are putting so much trust in the reader?

Sue: Not at all actually. *Follow Me to Ground* had been such a labour of love for so long and I had assumed it was not going to get published or read. I started working on *Follow Me to Ground* in 2013, and I had gotten a small bursary from the Arts Council, which covered my rent for six months. At the time, I was in my early 20's and I was working on correcting exam papers and doing my Masters in Visual Arts. My labour of love was this book. I decided I would present it as my final project for my Masters. I was then trying to get it published for years, trying to get interest, trying to get an agent, doing all the things I was told to do to make that happen, but they hadn't happened for me. So, when the publishing deal came about in a very contingent way, I felt huge hope and excitement. I really tried not to let myself get too invested before anything was signed. I didn't particularly like the idea of it getting slated, but I made my peace that that very well might happen and at the very least it would have some readers rather than zero readers.

Sinéad: I think it often takes indie publishers to give the bigger ones a kick up the bum. We saw it happen as well with *Notes to Self* by Emilie

Pine, originally published by Tramp Press before being picked up by Penguin. That's the great thing about Irish publishing, there is often a lot of trust and risk-taking involved.

Sue: I was trying to get published for years and had sent the first 1-30 pages of *Follow Me To Ground* to publishers and agents all over the world, and then it ended up being a guy down the road who said it should be in print. It taught me a lesson about my own writing and expectations.

Sinéad: You spoke earlier about how visual art influences your writing. Could you tell us a bit about that? How do you advise other writers to engage with other artforms?

Sue: My primary degree is in Art History and then I did an MA in Visual Art Practices, although I did it as an arts writer rather than an artist.
   There are other forms that strike me. I am very interested in knowledge and experiences that evade traditional or conventional expressive speech, and how they challenge a literary text and language. I'm very interested in other disciplines and other media that maybe have a more direct route to those kinds of experiences. Something like visual art, or something like film gets at your sematic knowledge and it's getting at your accrued experiences in a different way, in an arguably much more direct way. I think with visual art especially, it's been a part of my work life for a very long time and I'm very lucky that I got to study it and that I have a great facility for reading it and translating it to a degree, so it very much serves me when I'm thinking, "this sensation I'm after is not going to come to me in a literary text, but there's an artwork out that gets very close." So, the longer I spend time looking at that artwork, maybe something starts to bleed through into a piece of prose.
   With *Follow Me to Ground*, when looking at Ada, I was looking at the artist Jenny Keane. I read her PhD thesis cover to cover. She makes drawings that displace the horrific part of horror films by licking away the horrific element. She took a film still from a horror film, like *Interview with the Vampire*, where you have Kirsten Dunst with fang marks, and Jenny Keane licked away the fang marks from the drawing. Her saliva reacted with the Fabriano paper and left an organic gestating sore on the paper.

I got really fixated on that because she's recreating a horrific trope, but she's taking away the abject that's been pinned to the female body in a way that horror film often does quite liberally – it conflates the cis female body with vampirific or lupine impulses and bodily transformation. That was something that I wondered would serve me with this book.

Sinéad: It's also interesting that something so nurturing – licking someone clean – could become something monstrous, which is something you get at in *Follow Me to Ground*. Even though she's the healer, she's also this monstrous figure.

How do you go about planning and research? Is this something that comes naturally to you as someone who swallows up other artforms? Do you want to consume everything you can about the subject?

Sue: I'm quite lucky in that I was trained from a young age to be a voracious reader and to get excited by the scope of material available on any topic. Generally, if I'm at the outset of a book or if I have an idea, I'll start researching books that approach my themes in a similar way. Not necessarily through genre, but how subversive they are and how they work with images. It would be more technical than genre influenced. I would curate for myself a reading list and a selection of artists and films that I'll visually consume and research. Sometimes that would be a three-month turnaround, but I'll be writing alongside. Make your own reading list, don't read just what you think you should.

Sinéad: That's good advice because I think, particularly when it comes to longer projects, writers can get quite bogged down in the research. Maybe it's one of those rules of writing that is often miscommunicated; research should not be a chore, but part of the process. When you are obsessed with a subject, the research is fun and interesting, and you have subconsciously been doing it for a while already.

Please talk us through your writing routine and how it looks now in comparison to before you had your first book deal.

Sue: Since about 2016, I've been writing full time. It didn't always look very pretty in the early days. I would always get up and try to get to my desk as early as possible in the morning. On a good day, I'd get up by 6 or 6:30 and start writing by 7:30. I'd be working on a commission or some sort of collaborative text or a body of research, whereas now I frontload the fiction because I feel I get my best writing done in the morning. Jeff VanderMeer has spoken about how the uncanny is still with you in the morning. The dreamworld is lingering a bit more richly the closer you are to dawn.

I'll write the most pressing thing in the morning, and then whatever is more externally facing, like commissions or freelance or prepping teaching is what I'll do after lunch. And then I'll work on the things that don't require me to be as internal or forget the world as much. I've been hugely fortunate this year because I got an Arts Council bursary, and I was awarded residency at UCD. So, this year I've been working on a new project non-stop pretty exclusively, and I haven't had to divide the day between fiction and freelance, or whatever it is.

My routine is always getting up as early as possible and doing something to ground myself. I might meditate or I would go for a run, take out a tarot card – something just to clear my head enough that I'm in my body and not in the world so I can write or edit as consistently as I can. I usually run out of steam between 12 or 2pm and take an hour's break, run some errands. By the time I come back to my desk, all of that internal logic has kind of dissipated, because the rules of the real world have crept in. But I'm primed then to do another kind of work, which is more research or structural work, rather than writing out sentences.

A friend of mine told me about the Pomodoro method and there are definitely days where I do that. But mostly, especially on residency, I get that magic feeling of spending a window of time so immersed in the writing. But that's incredibly lofty and I wouldn't encourage trying to reach for that on a daily basis because it's not realistic or sustainable. It feels otherworldly because it's a different type of attention.

Lewis Hyde wrote in the *The Gift* about the sense of something coming to you or something coming in and taking over, and that the writing is this gift of inspiration. But I think there are ways you can control it or instigate it with triggers. When I'm reading, I'm looking for something that is simply so resonant that I have to write. I was reading Kate Zambreno's *Drifts* and she writes about coming across Rilke and how Rilke's blood cancer was galvanised by pricking his finger on a rose, and how he died by a rose. The idea of a new form of caress and the tactility of the petal got me writing for an hour that day.

Sometimes you're reading or watching or looking and nothing comes for days at a time, and then you're looking for a new kind of discipline to sustain you during that period. I have to know that those periods have happened before and that they've ended. I wrote this essay called 'On Formative Reading' which details the idea that as a writer you are always working if you are reading deeply and meaningfully. If the writing isn't happening, you always have reading. Throw yourself with as much energy as possible into the reading. Don't be a passive reader, but an engaged, volatile, and questioning reader. That's feeding the same part of the brain. I know that's what will get me out of it eventually.

Sinéad: What is your experience with rejection and how do you deal with it?

Sue: You get the straightforward rejections and they're fine. There were times when friends would put me in touch with an agent, and the agent would ask to see some of the novel and then they'd ask to see more of the novel, and *then* they'd reject it. That was harder at first to make peace with because I'd ask myself, "when is it ever going to happen?"

But going back to the manuscript, I'd read the first few pages and think, "I like this book and it is doing what I want it to do." That had to be enough to sustain me. I really loved these sentences that I'd managed to put together and I really loved this character, Ada. I had written a book that I wanted to read. So, I think you do need a lot of internally generated sustenance.

Listening to authors I really admire talk about their experiences with rejection certainly helped me a lot. And it's important to take things with a pinch of salt. I'd been trying with *Follow Me to Ground* for so long, and then the way it happened was so contingent, and then it got picked up by a bigger publisher in the UK and the States. But you have to keep your head on your shoulders. You can't let your ego take over either.

There were certainly times when I conflated the rejections with the quality of my work, and then I stopped myself doing that.

Sinéad: Did you feel that the book would still be complete if it were never published?

Sue: It's such a funny thing when your first book comes out. *Follow Me to Ground* did feel complete to me, and people giving me feedback and writing reviews felt so strange because I knew this book backwards and it has existed in my world for a very long time so to experience it anew or talk anew about it was quite a challenge. But it had felt very complete.

Sinéad: I think it's difficult when submitting to recognise when you need to take a step back from your work, or if you should keep working on it until someone wants it. How do you know when the time to step back is?

Sue: I've been very lucky with the editors I've worked with and my agent Lucy Luck. The editorial feedback is there. The editor is there to amplify the writer's voice and suggest to them the edits the author could make. When I'm giving feedback, I have to ask myself, "what does this story need that the writer is equipped to give it?" You know as a writer when that kind of edit is being suggested to you. If it feels outlandish to you, it's not a goer.

Sinéad: What would your final piece of advice be to writers at any stage, whether they have the work and want to submit it, or they have the idea and they want to get started?

Sue: In terms of how to get writing, find texts and stories that not only inspire you but make you reconfigure your relationship with the world and yourself. Find books that rewrite your insides. It can take a while to find a writer who does that to you, but typically when you find one you have two or three, because they have their own set of influences. That, to me, has gotten me writing. A feeling beyond excitement and discovery. There's another set of experiences that you can and will access if only you could just hang on another minute inside this sentence. Take relish in that feeling. Remind yourself how high the stakes can be, and how glorious it is to spend time with literature in that way. Your experience with the writing alone in a room has to be enough.

In terms of getting published, when I first realised that I was going to get published – it was a shock to realise that what people were drawn to was the weirdest shit. It was the kind of stuff that, had I ever dreamed that a publisher would look at it years ago, I would have taken out because wouldn't have had as much faith in myself. It's so hard being a writer, especially on social media, to think that you've anything to offer that hasn't been done to death. So don't be afraid to be incredibly nuanced and specific; trends will change, audiences will change. You have to write what you have within you at the time and the audience will come when it comes. The audience might be fifty people, it could be tens of thousands. Let all those other things fall into place.

If you start writing with any kind of agenda other than making a mark that pleases you on the page at that moment, then you're only doing a disservice.

My books are so strange and they aren't bestsellers, which is something I was never after, but I have my readers now and that has changed my life. I have the most beautiful, devout, enthusiastic readers, which is something I hadn't dreamed of before.

Sinéad: Thank you so much for talking with me, Sue. I've certainly felt really inspired listening to you, and I hope it will help a lot of emerging writers.

ABOUT THE CONTRIBUTORS

Martins Deep

Martins Deep (he/him) is an Urhobo poet based in Zaria. He is a photographer, digital artist, & currently an undergraduate student of Ahmadu Bello University, Zaria.

Sue Rainsford

Sue Rainsford is an Irish fiction and arts writer based in Dublin. A graduate of Trinity College, IADT, and Bennington College, she is a recipient of the VAI/DCC Art Writing Award, the Arts Council Literature Bursary Award, and a MacDowell Fellowship. She has been awarded residencies by such institutions as the Irish Museum of Modern Art and Maynooth University, and recent commissions include RTÉ Radio 1 and BBC Radio 4. Her début novel, *Follow Me to Ground*, was originally published by New Island Books in Ireland, where it received the Kate O'Brien Award, was long-listed for the Desmond Elliott Prize and the Republic of Consciousness Award when it was published in the UK by Doubleday, and received starred reviews from *Kirkus Reviews* and *Publishers Weekly* when it was released in the US by Scribner. Her short story, "Shorn", was a finalist for the 2021 New York Radio Festival Awards. Most recently, her second novel, *Redder Days*, was published in Ireland and the UK by Doubleday in 2021, and she was appointed Writer in Residence at UCD for 2022.

Kirsten Mosher

Kirsten Mosher is a visual artist and writer living in Western Massachusetts. Her project *Soul Mate 180°* for which she received the LACMA Art+Technology Award, was exhibited at the Los Angeles County Museum of Art in 2020. Her booklet *Zero (minutes to) Home*, a short story in ten flashes, was published with *Selektion*, Frankfurt, Germany in 2021. Her stories have been published in *Ellipsis Zine*, Volume Five of *The Bath*

Flash Fiction Anthology, 2020, and Issue 6 of *The Cormorant Broadsheet, 2021* among others. Her series, *Automotive Stories*, occasionally shows up in the Automotive sections of local newspapers.

Patrick Kruth

Patrick Kruth is a writer from Ireland. His work has previously been published in *Hypertext Magazine* and is upcoming in the *Between These Shores Annual*.

Kayla King

Kayla King has been making up stories since her freshman year in high school. She graduated with her Bachelor's Degree in English from Boise State University in 2013 and is currently working on her MFA and teaching at Texas State University. Her work has previously appeared in *Defunkt Magazine* and *Voidspa,ce Zine*. She can be found on Twitter @kaylaisshining, where her tweets are sometimes as surreal as her prose.

Sam Martone

Sam Martone lives and writes in New York City

Aisling Cahill

Aisling Cahill is a chronically ill and disabled creator from New Ross, Co. Wexford. Her work plays with the interaction between words and lens-based imagery and explores themes of the body, the natural world, and the unreliable shadow of memory.

E J Delaney

E J Delaney is a writer living in Brisbane, Australia's River City. E J's short stories have appeared in *Daily Science Fiction* and the podcasts, *Cast of Wonders* and *Escape Pod*, as well as in limited edition print collections from Air & Nothingness Press. E J also writes for younger readers, contributing to the Australian school magazines *Countdown*, *Blast Off* and *Touchdown*, the American school magazine *Spider*, and the French periodical *Short Circuit*, which is dispensed worldwide by way of free-standing tickertape machines. E J's poetry features in the Irish teen and young adult literary journal *Paper Lanterns*.

Ian Ledward

Ian lives in Fife, working as a professional artist. He aims to bring his experience in visual symbolism to the written word, and the themes of Time and Change often feature in his work.

His writing is sometimes humorous, sometimes introspective and is a continuing journey of discovery. Both poems and fiction offer the reader an opportunity to explore ideas and places they may not have visited.

He gained a distinction from the Open University in Creative Writing, is an active member of the Open University Poets' Society, and has work published in various magazines and anthologies.

Chris Kuriata

Chris Kuriata lives in the Niagara region of Canada. His short fiction focuses on a cast of diverse characters, including a middle-aged female amateur stand-up comic, a ghost-hunting massage parlour attendant, an elderly poisoner, and a woman capable of translating the dead. These characters and stories explore issues of gentrification, sex trade, Canadian-US border relations, and factory farming. He can be found on twitter @CKuriata

Epiphany Ferrell

Epiphany Ferrell lives on the edge of the Shawnee Forest in Southern Illinois, USA. Her stories appear in more than 60 journals and anthologies, including *Bending Genres*, *The Molotov Cocktail*, *Best Microfictions*, *Best Small Fictions*, and other places. She is a two-time Pushcart nominee, and a past recipient of the *Prime Number Magazine* Flash Fiction Prize. She's on Facebook and Twitter, and at epiphanyferrell.com

Justin Clement

Justin is a storytelling artist, exploring life's meanings and methods. Writing both literary and speculative fiction, he's an alumnus of the Purple Hibiscus Trust Creative Writing Workshop facilitated by Chimamanda Ngozi Adichie, and he's also the recipient of the 2020 Gulliver Travel Grant awarded by the Speculative Literature Foundation. He's been a finalist for the African Writers Award, The Afritondo Short Story Prize, and The Toyin Falola Prize. His fiction appears in two print anthologies, *Water*

Birds on the Lakeshore and *The Hope, The Prayer, The Anthem*. He posts some things on Instagram @a.certain.justin

Sahar Ahmed

Sahar Ahmed (she/her) is from Lahore, Pakistan, where she worked as a Barrister for many years, and between all the time spent in London and now Dublin (where she works as an academic), she no longer knows what's 'home'. She is fat, she is Brown, and is deeply committed to the idea of a future where Black and Brown people do not need to do ‹anti-racist work› in order to survive.

Olivia Payne

Olivia Payne is a librarian working in London. She is an alumnus of the Faber Academy and proud member of the Write Like a Grrrl community. She has previously had work published or forthcoming in *Litro Magazine*, *STORGY*, *The Amphibian Literary Journal*, *Cobra Milk*, *Ellipsis Zine*, *Corporeal*, and *Alphabet Box*. She is currently working on her first novel.

Justin Rigamonti

Justin Rigamonti teaches writing at two colleges in Portland, Oregon and serves as Program Coordinator for Portland Community College's Carolyn Moore Writing Residency, the first writing residency of its kind hosted by a community college in the United States (@cmwritershouse on Instagram). His poetry has been recently published by or is forthcoming in *American Poetry Review*, *New Ohio Review*, *Radar*, *Cimarron*, and *Smartish Pace*.

Lea Mc Carthy

Lea McCarthy is a 24-year-old LGBT writer from Sligo. She has a degree in Creative Writing from NUIG. Lea was the winner of the Morning Coffee writing prize 2020 and was shortlisted for the Redline Poetry Prize 2022. She has previously had work published in *Sonder*, *Ropes*, *Paper Lanterns*, and she has written the screenplay of a film that was screened at Fresh Film Fest. In her everyday life, she manages storytelling and creative writing projects in Italian primary schools. Lea has recently completed her first novel and is editing it furiously.

Don Noel

Don Noel is retired from four decades' prizewinning print and broadcast journalism in the United States. He took an MBA from Fairfield University in Connecticut at age 81, and has in the decade since published more than 100 short stories or other pieces, all of which can be read at his blog, dononoel.com.

Claire O'Brien

Claire is a singer and songwriter from Cork, now living in Glasgow. Graduating with an MA in songwriting from UL, she returned to Cork to teach piano in September 2019 only for the pandemic to strike the following March. Without the option of teaching or live performance, her focus turned to prose writing. Her first piece of non-fiction work, 'Daughters, was published online after it placed runner up in the All Ireland Scholarship Creative writing competition 2021. After completing the Stinging Fly Summer School with author Sinead Gleeson in Summer 2022, Claire developed this piece, 'Tides'.

Robert Coakley

Robert Coakley is from Wexford, Ireland. His work has appeared in *The Wexford Bohemian*. He is a recent graduate of UCD's Masters in Creative Writing and a recipient of the Agility Award 2022 from the Arts Council.

Cian Dunne

Cian Dunne has recently graduated from a degree in English and Russian at Trinity College Dublin. In his final year, he edited the Trinity *Journal of Literary Translation*. He lives in Westport, Co. Mayo, where he keeps himself busy, never being bored.

Isa Robertson

Isa's first short story was composed at age three and concerned a baby black bear's somewhat possessive relationship with a roll of toilet paper. His first science fiction novel, Whirlo-Wormhole, was started at age eight (under great secrecy) as a birthday present for his brother and featured interdimensional crocodiles. His first chemistry textbook, Backyard Bangs, was started at age twelve, to chronicle his favourite methods for making things go *Boom!* He started writing about amateur neuroscience in his late teens, and mysticism in his early twenties. What he will do next is hard to predict. isarobertson.com

Colm Brennan

Colm Brennan is a full time writer of poetry and fiction. His work has appeared in *Poetry Ireland Review*, *The Cormorant Broadsheet*, *The Ogham Stone*, and *Profiles*. He was a shortlisted poet in the Red Line Festival poetry competition 2022 and has an MA in Creative Writing from UL.

Valerie Hunter

Valerie Hunter teaches high school English and has an MFA in writing for children and young adults from Vermont College of Fine Arts. Her work has appeared in publications including *Paper Lanterns*, *Wizards in Space*, *Beneath Ceaseless Skies*, *The Quiet Reader*, and *Room*.